STILL A COUNTRY BOY

After Embracing the World

A Memoir

LOREN FINNELL

Mayhaven Publishing, Inc.
P O Box 557
Mahomet, IL 61853
USA

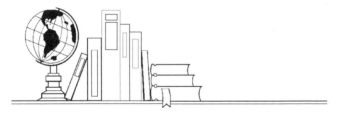

Cover Design: Doris Replogle Wenzel
Copyright © 2011 Loren Finnell
First Edition—First Printing, December, 2011
Library of Congress Control Number: 2011943657
ISBN 13: 978 193227884-2
ISBN 10: 193227884-2

We want to thank all those who provided photos for this book.
And we thank the various publications for the use of their articles and
documents.

Lovingly Dedicated

To my devoted partner of forty-five wonderful years.

11/18/14
FOR JANE —
WITH WARM REGARDS!
Bill

Left: Loren Finnell, Executive Director of the Resource Foundation, being presented the *National Peace Corps Association's 2006 Sargent Shriver Award for Distinguished Humanitarian Service*, by Harris Wofford, co-founder of the Peace Corps with Sargent Shriver and former Senator from Pennsylvania.

Many Thanks To

Darryl Hunt, long-time friend and current Secretary of the Board of Directors of The Resource Foundation, who graciously agreed to edit out all of the typos and poorly constructed sentences that I managed to include in the original document, as well as make important changes to the content and overall presentation.

Thanks also to the following friends and colleagues who read the original draft and offered their opinions and suggestions, pointed out errors and omissions, supplied additional information, and basically improved upon that which I had produced: George Baker (Ecuador PCV 1964-66), Tad Baldwin (Ecuador PCV 1963-65), Alain Concher, John Coyne (Ethiopia PCV 1962-64), Jose M. de Lasa, Enrique Fernandez, Pilar Finnell, Tom Fox (Togo PC Staff 1965-67), Rev. Alberto Jimenez S.J., Sandra Larriva, Julia Love, Marcela Lopez-Macedonio, Kris and Stella Merschrod, Bill Moody, Cristian Ossa, Ken Ricci (Colombia PCV 1965-66), and Todd Tibbals (Peru PCV 1962-64).

And further thanks to the friends, family, and colleagues who provided much appreciated encouragement that helped motivate me to finish this project: Rosa Baker (Ecuador PC Training Instructor 1964), Ron and Vera Bertagnoli, Jovita Castillo, John Childress, Ken (Ecuador PCV 1963-65) and Jane (Ecuador 1964-65) Cole, David and Anne Cook, Fabian and Leny Cordova, Frank and Alina Diaz-Balart, Phyllis DiMenna, Sheldon and Phyllis Evans, Sabrina Ferrisi, Lorena Finnell, Carolyn Gallaher (Colombia PCV 1965-67), Robert Glickman, Bruce Gottschall (Peru PCV 1965-67), Rafael Guardans, Bill Hockman, Ruedi Laager, Carol Wilson-Lark (Ecuador PCV 1964-66), Clemente and Emeratriz Machuca, Peter Markey, Jean and Gisele Masse, Tiphaine and Olivia Masse, Colleen May, David McKenzie, Cristian A. Ossa, Kathryn Playa, Larry and Judy Prince, Alison Rende, Federico and Carmen Gloria Riesco, Brooks Smith, Jo Young Switzer, Sheila Tiarks (Ecuador PCV 1964-66), and Maria Eugenia Vasquez.

Contents

Foreword

by Senator Harris Wofford

We all have stories to tell, but most of us never roll them into one ball and publish them. We're lucky that Loren Finnell has done that because his heart-warming story is interesting, important, and encouraging.

From his country-boy beginnings through his character-building early schooling in high school and college, through his career-shaping experience in the Peace Corps, and his successful 47-year work in international development, crowned by the founding and leadership of the Resource Foundation for a quarter of a century, his life is the kind of success story that is good for young and old to read. It is also an entertaining tale.

He tells of the hard times his parents suffered and how he and his sister learned self-reliance while they were living in a one-room cabin in a rural area along the Rock River, near Dixon, Illinois.

In third grade, he learned that if he wanted money to spend he had to earn it. For three years in elementary school he delivered, on his bike, 80 papers each morning. From high school on, he was on his own— "The child is father to the man."

From that start, he takes us through surprising moments with lasting impact—when the Manchester Church of the Brethren's Director of Christian Education, whom he hardly knew, wrote him a penned letter saying, "You have always impressed me as a very fine young man... You always walk tall and straight—I admire that... I expect something significant from you....God has need of such as you." It would help change his life.

Soon after that, he heard about Kennedy's idea of the Peace Corps and after graduating from college, he began his adventures as a Peace Corps Volunteer in Mexico and Ecuador, and traveled on to Asia, Africa and Latin America, with assignments in South America and Indo-China. He later founded The Resource Foundation, built it into the multi-million dollar venture it is today, and had great occasions when his work was honored, including the halls of Congress where I first met him.

In the grand Senate Caucus Room, in which both John and Robert Kennedy launched their presidential campaigns, I had the privilege of presenting Loren with the 2006 Sargent Shriver Humanitarian Award, on behalf of the National Peace Corps Association. This award was seconded warmly that afternoon by former Peace Corps Volunteer Senator Chris Dodd.

In nominating Loren, Tom Fox, a respected leader in international development, wrote that [Finnell], "can take considerable credit for the U.S. development community's acceptance of the fact that development will remain very slow in many poor countries if their own civil society is not empowered and supported, through the vehicle of NGOs" and that "Finnell's Resource Foundation has both encouraged and helped many individual and corporate donors support non-U.S. NGOs in ways they previously felt was too complicated or risky." He said Loren has really "written the book" on this practice, "a huge accomplishment."

Loren has indeed written, and written well, that book. The devil, and also everything good is, of course, in the details. The only deviltry Loren confesses, with some pleasure, is that in his first days in Bozeman, Montana, for Peace Corps training to work alongside agricultural extension workers in Ecuador, he had his first taste of beer. He was a teetotaler who had rarely been outside of North Manchester, Indiana, a dry town, and had been brought up in the Church of the Brethren, with two Brethren preachers as grandfathers and a father who later became one. But he didn't want to be anti-social in training, or in his life in Ecuador, so at the end of rugged 6 a.m. to 9 p.m. training days he joined the other volunteers at the Hofbrauhaus a few blocks away.

With far more manifest pleasure he tells how during his two-year tour in Ecuador he fell in love with, and after some ups and downs, married Pilar: "So there we were, united and ready to face the world. I was a Protestant, reserved, a time freak, a tosser and a country boy. Pilar was a Catholic, outgoing, always late, a saver and into the arts." With the language and culture issues, "no one thought we had a chance to make it, but here we are 45 years later."

Looking back on his life trajectory, Loren says "the single most important event was the birth of the Peace Corps in late 1961." Hearing about that birth, "it was impossible to ignore the excitement being generated by this new opportunity. I knew immediately that it was something that I wanted to do." When he was accepted and left for the Peace Corps, he did not realize he was starting a career that would take him around the world and make multiple trips to 44 countries in three continents, and enable him "to assist millions of persons living in poverty, both directly and indirectly."

He had "never been on such an adventure." In fact, he says he had never really been outside of North Manchester, Indiana, or interacted with persons from another country or culture. Reflecting on how he matured during the two years in Ecuador, he writes that most of all he, "had to come face to face and deal with a level of poverty that far outstripped even the very difficult times that my own family had experienced." It had a deep impact on him and, he says, "made me more committed than ever about what I wanted to do with the rest of my life."

Soon after Loren returned from Ecuador, President Lyndon Johnson called the Peace Corps "a training ground for Great Citizens." In Loren's story, it is evident that he has been for half a century and is now a Great Citizen, not only of the United States of America but above all as a citizen of the world.

A wise philosopher and observer of America and of the world, Scott Buchanan of St. John's College, said that the watch words for the 20th century were: "We must be more inventive if we are going to do our duty. For a lot of that century, and fortunately still at work in the 21st century, Loren

Finnell has been inventive in the best sense.

Buchanan was the Socratic teacher who most stirred and stretched my view of the world and sent me forth on an adventure in India, studying Gandhi in the year after he was killed. I was then at about the same age as Loren Finnell when he set forth in the Peace Corps. Buchanan left me with other watchwords that he considered the main advice of Socrates: "Follow the question where it leads." This book shows how Loren has been doing that well, and it has already led to many good things, including this book.

I hope this "country boy's" book will be widely read and stir the imagination of those who are ready to go on their own adventure—at home or around the world.

Harris Wofford was elected to the U.S. Senate in a 1991 special Pennsylvania election that made national and international news. However he is better known for being one of the founders of the Peace Corps, as well as a special assistant to President John F. Kennedy. During the decade of struggle from Montgomery to Memphis, he was an advisor to Martin Luther King, Jr. He wrote extensively about his experiences in his 1980 book entitled, *Of Kennedys and Kings*.

Introduction

Mostly due to my wife Pilar's urgings, I decided to commit to paper some of my experiences during, what has been to this point, a 47-year career in the international development arena. It is prefaced by a description of what led me to get involved in a career of this nature.

I took on this task, convinced that what I have to say may not be of interest to anyone beyond my immediate family and a few friends. However, those who do choose to take the time to read it may come away with a better understanding of what moved me to leave the comfort zone of my youth, and how I subsequently adjusted to and embraced many new and strange environs, while not allowing the country to be left behind.

In addition to my general upbringing, there were a number of important factors that helped shape my life. One of the most significant of these took place in November of 1961—during my sophomore year of college. I received an unsolicited letter in the mail from Ruth Graham, the Manchester Church of the Brethren Director of Christian Education. Although I knew who she was, I had not interacted with her very much, as I rarely went to church there, anymore, as church services became available on campus. Nevertheless, she penned a beautiful note praising me, indicating she "expected something significant..." from me. I was really taken by that, and I'm sad to admit that I never said anything to her. While no one who knows me today will believe it, I was extremely shy during my youth, and I just couldn't bring myself to approach her, but what she wrote, along with other events, and the birth of the Peace Corps at a time when I was looking for something to "hang my hat on," had a major impact on determining the path

I would take in life and the role I was to play in the international development arena.

My travels in Latin America, Africa, and Asia would eventually bring me to the suburbs of New York City, where I established a nonprofit agency in the basement of my Larchmont home—thanks to the support and encouragement of my Ecuadorean wife Pilar, a "souvenir" of my Peace Corps days.

The Resource Foundation pioneered a new and effective way to approach international development, one that focuses on the overwhelming importance of the role of local nonprofit agencies, and it continues to be a unique response to "need" situations and a successful method to involve both beneficiaries and donors. Now in its 24th year, The Resource Foundation is annually channeling approximately $10.0 million to some 175 local NGOs (non-governmental organizations) located in 25 Latin American and Caribbean countries. For the past four years, Charity Navigator, has given The Resource Foundation its highest 4-Star rating—something only 8% of nonprofit organizations achieve.

The Resource Foundation highlights the generosity and outreach of major corporations and other donors, and reports on the meaningful work of the NGOs, while managing to build a solid reputation within the development community.

The journey described in the pages ahead will trace my personal development and provide the raison d'etre for founding The Resource Foundation. But before I take you around the world with me, I think it's important to share some influences that made me who I am today.

Along the way, I hope to offer a few thoughts about what I have learned—for whatever they may be worth. None of them are earthshaking, but those related to the second half of my professional career—The Resource Foundation—have been classified as innovative and groundbreaking by independent observers.

I

The First Years

1942-1954

Very few country boys are born in Cook County Hospital in Chicago, Illinois, but my sister Anne Marie was born there in 1937, and I followed five years later—on July 3, 1942. My parents both grew up in rural Indiana. I, too, would end up there soon enough and become deeply entrenched, feeling comfortable with the simple life style that characterized North Manchester, Indiana, though I was not destined to join the majority of my high-school classmates who still reside there or who live within shouting distance. I had the privilege of being selected to travel the world and work on behalf of those less fortunate. I would be drawn away physically, but I would never lose sight of who I was inside—a simple country boy from Indiana.

My father Ralph Theodore had moved to Chicago in 1933, along with my mother Vera Elizabeth Hartsough, to obtain a graduate degree at the Church of the Brethren Seminary. In spite of garnering the highest grades in the history of that institution, he decided instead to go into personnel work with Sears. It wasn't until many years later (circa 1980) that he finally made use of his training and began preaching in one-room country churches in the Blue Ridge Mountains of Virginia, two hours south of Washington D.C. My mother held many interesting jobs over the years, including a reporter for a major newspaper in Rockford, Illinois, but her calling was in the area of education. Later in life she would obtain a Masters degree and teach high-school Home Economics.

I believe that it's also worth mentioning that both my grandfathers were preachers, Grandpa Hartsough in North Manchester, Indiana, at one of the largest Brethren churches in the U.S., and my Grandpa Finnell, traveling widely from church to church in the Midwest to preach the gospel and speak out for abstinence. At some point, the latter became a candidate for Governor of the State of Indiana and, later, President of the United States, representing the Prohibition Party. Obviously, he was not successful in either case. Equally obvious, in terms of my own life's work, is the fact that I was not swayed into being a third-generation pastor, nor did I choose to become a teetotaler.

From Chicago, my father's employment in personnel work and sales took us to Decatur (1943) and then on to the outskirts of Dixon (1945), both in Illinois, where our first residence was a one-room cabin in a nearby rural area along the Rock River. I was not yet of school age, but I do remember my mother pulling me down a dirt road in a red wagon so that we could take my sister to attend a one-room school. Our cabin had no central heating and our food was kept in an icebox. We had no telephone.

We soon moved into Dixon proper, and stayed until I had completed sixth grade. We lived in four different, modest homes during that time, and we attended a small Brethren Church on the other side of the river from where we resided. My other memories of Dixon include walking the five blocks to kindergarten by myself every day—something that was not uncommon during those days.

As my parents couldn't afford multiply bikes, my first bicycle was a full-size Schwinn—even though I was short in stature. I learned to ride with no seat—sitting on the bar—and continued to do so even after I was big enough to have the seat affixed. My father told me early on that if I wanted money, I would have to work for it. So in the third grade, I got a paper route, and for the next three years I folded and delivered, on my bike, 80 papers each morning prior to school and on weekends. I also collected for those every Saturday. I was responsible for paying the newspaper company, keeping a record of my finances and doing my own banking. I used part of my earnings to purchase our family's first television set—a black and white of course, and it served us well for the next dozen years.

I never viewed the one-room cabin, the responsibility of walking to school alone, the outsized bicycle, nor the paper route as a burden or exceptional. I would not have wanted it to be any other way, because my life was very positively influenced by those experiences, my family surroundings, my formal and non-formal education, and the value systems I was born into and taught. The fact that I was given significant responsibilities at an early age prepared me for dealing with critical situations later in life. And I am deeply indebted to my parents for the loving manner in which I was raised and for the support I was given during their entire lives.

Anne, Dad, and me on Easter Sunday, 1945—Rock River Cabin.

II

Changes and Character Building

Junior High and High School

1954-1960

Our family moved to North Manchester, Indiana, during the summer of 1954, at a time when the billboard outside of town indicated that it was "the home of 4,377 contented citizens and a few old soreheads." Soon after it was erected, the few old soreheads made them take it down. It was a quiet, rural community that catered to the many farmers in the area. There were no stoplights on Main Street. The business area encompassed a mere three blocks, but in addition to the few storefronts, there was one small industry in town that made school furniture, there was also a retirement home, and Manchester College, all of which provided employment opportunities. There were no dial phones. Live operators would connect you to the three-digit telephone number you requested, but they could just as easily have done so if you gave them the person's name.

The majority of the farmers in the area were Quakers, Old Order Brethren, Mennonites, and Amish, primarily producing corn, wheat and alfalfa, or raising dairy cows, pigs or poultry.

My parents were returning to their roots to take over a small, neighborhood grocery store and meat-processing business where customers could rent storage areas to keep their frozen food. We lived in the attached house.

Both sets of my grandparents lived in North Manchester at that time as well.

Since I was going into junior high and did not feel particularly attached to Dixon, I viewed the transition as an adventure. My sister, who was between her junior and senior years of high school, had left many friends behind and did not share my enthusiasm.

But I was at an age when new hormones begin to kick in, and the girls in North Manchester viewed me as new territory. They thought I was "cute," and I was very popular with them for awhile, but I was too shy to take advantage of it. Unfortunately, their attention made me unpopular with the guys, who saw me as a threat. After the dust settled things were pretty normal and I began to fit in. Moreover, since I grew from 4'11" to 6'2" in a period of less than two years, I quickly lost my "cuteness." The spurt in growth did, however, enhance my ability to be involved in basketball, football and baseball, all of which I lettered in.

The "urban" school I attended consolidated with the "rural" school during my time. There were about 80 students in my graduating class. The majority of them still live in, or are within shouting distance of, North Manchester. Our family attended the Church of the Brethren, where my Grandfather Hartsough had previously been the pastor, and religion was an important part of our life. In addition to helping out at the grocery store whenever I was needed, I spent all of my summers mowing lawns, tending to chickens and turkeys on several farms and baling hay with a farmer, who contracted himself out to a large number of his neighbors.

Like many "mom and pop" businesses, the grocery store progressively fell on hard times over the years we were in North Manchester. It finally succumbed to a large supermarket that was built on the edge of town. My folks had to declare bankruptcy, resulting in a move to a smaller home. Money was hard to come by. They couldn't even afford to give me the $1.25 per week it cost to eat in the high-school. I began covering this, as well as paying for all of my own clothes and other out-of-pocket expenses. Since I was accustomed to finding odd jobs, these changes were all taken in stride.

What was a bit tougher to accept was the day my mother told me that she and dad were splitting up. I still have vivid memories of the very short, one-sided conversation the two of us had at the kitchen table, followed by several hours of shooting hoops in the back yard while trying to figure things out for myself.

The breakup was obviously a product of the stress created by losing the store and their economic situation. It came midway through my senior year of high school. My mother went to live with her sister in Grand Rapids, Michigan, but luckily the separation didn't last long. My parents reunited and would live to celebrate 50 years of marriage.

What did happen, however, was that immediately after my high-school graduation—literally—in 1960, my parents went to live in Chicago, where my father had found a job as a salesman with Dun & Bradstreet. I didn't follow them to Chicago, and that left me to fend for myself at the tender age of 18. Although I went home for occasional visits, never again did the three of us live under the same roof on a permanent basis, and I was financially independent from that moment on.

There were lots of lessons learned during this part of my life—others were reinforced. The need to work in order to have money in my pocket was of course not new to me. However, the need to make enough money to help the family survive put a new twist on things. It went well beyond just buying my own soda pop and candy bars, and paying for my own gasoline. Having to ask the mother of some of my friends to assist with my laundry taught me a bit about humility, and placed a value on what real friendship and caring meant. Family values also came into play during this stage of my life. We had been a close-knit family. We played together, we prayed together, and we worked together. Even when the short separation happened, the extended family came together to aid in the healing process, but while I had always been quite self-sufficient and had made a lot of decisions on my own, the abruptness of being pushed out on my own accelerated my independence.

Years later, in 1979, and my parents moved to a lovely two-bedroom cabin in the woods near tiny Kinderhook, Virginia, when my father finally decided to preach. After helping with the transition over a several-day period, my wife, daughter and I went to Sunday church service with them. There couldn't have been more than 15-20 persons attending, swelled by the five of us, and all went well until it came time to sing. My daughter Lorena, who was nine at the time, was used to Catholic ceremonies, where very few people raise their voice in song, so when a quartet got up in front of the church and started singing "Amazing Grace" in their twangy southern harmony—backed up by a steel guitar—it was all Pilar and I could do to keep her from laughing, but it was music and a group of people we would all learn to love and appreciate as time went by.

Me, first-row center, with our Manchester, Indiana,
high-school baseball team.

Manchester College

Manchester, Indiana

1960-1964

The decision to go on to college was not made until the very final weeks of high school. I had no interest in continuing my education, in spite of the fact that Grandfather Hartsough, both of my parents, eight of my aunts and uncles and my sister Anne, had all graduated from Manchester College. I don't remember having any particular idea about what I was going to do during the next phase of my life, but I had no incentive to study any further. Moreover, my parents were not pressuring me, as they were preoccupied with the status of their marriage and their economic situation.

Thank goodness there were some cooler heads who helped change my mind. I had been a good student in high school, and there were several teachers who began to encourage me to go on with my education. The same can be said for a number of my close friends, and their parents. Application processes were much simpler at that time, and I was, of course, well-known by the College officials—from the President on down. So once I made the decision to go to college, it was easy to move ahead.

My only challenge was finances. Since I'd been helping out at home, I had very little savings, and scholarships were few and far between. Nevertheless, I managed. I was forced to sell the 1929 mint-condition Model A Ford that I had bought from a neighbor for $75 several years earlier. I sold it for $250 and have regretted it ever since. I also got a full-time gardening

22

job at the College for the summer, and I started working evenings and weekends at a neighborhood grocery store that had survived. It was hand to mouth, but I did it.

In fact, I paid for my entire four-year college education, something that is nearly impossible these days. I continued to work 30-40 hours a week at the grocery store, even during the school year, while taking a full load of classes and playing football during the Fall. Unfortunately, I had to give up basketball and baseball. I did a variety of things during the summers, including construction work on a high-rise apartment building on Lake Shore Drive in Chicago. I also managed, and cooked, for a drive-in hamburger place in North Manchester. Bottom line—I graduated without a penny of debt.

That first summer, when I was left to fend for myself, I lived in the basement of my grandma Hartsough's home. She regularly rented out the second floor to college students during the school year, and when my parents moved, they gave her several pieces of furniture, including my own bed and dresser. Given my economic situation, and the fact that I was sleeping in my own bed, you would have thought that I would have had a free ride. Wrong! I paid rent. She did give me a meal or two once in a while, but I mostly ate at the homes of some of my friends, or bought something cheap, like a McDonalds.

When school started in the fall, I had the good fortune to live in a house near the campus that was owned by the parents of one of the students. There were no fraternities, but this was the closest thing to one. The dorms were full, and the College needed the extra space. Fifteen or so of us were handpicked because they trusted us to behave. I guess I had a reputation of being a straight arrow type of guy. Imagine that! This arrangement lasted the entire four years.

Manchester College is a liberal arts college, where you get a taste of everything: art, music, science, math, history, languages, but I had no clue about what to major in as I had never really been pushed to think about it. An aptitude test that I had taken earlier indicated that I seemed to be good

Loren Finnell

with numbers and was organized. Since one of the strong points of the College was economics and accounting—the others were education and pre-med—I chose that since I had no interest in any of the other areas.

I quickly found out that college is not as easy as high school. While I had been nearly a straight-A student in high school, without putting in much effort, I soon learned that I was going to have to change my ways. When I got a "D" on my first essay in English class, I requested a meeting with my professor and asked her how I could raise my grade. She told me in no uncertain terms that I would have to improve the quality of my work—and the grade would be a by-product. How quaint! I made the effort and, while I did not set the world afire, I did manage to attain a "B" average. But most importantly, I actually did learn a thing or two. It also helped me be selected a member of *Who's Who Among American Colleges and Universities* during my senior year, based on my grades, my extracurricular activities and the votes of my peers and my professors.

There were a number of important things that helped shape my life. Almost all of these took place during my college years. In addition to the flattering letter I received during my sophomore year (1961), a major event also occurred in Washington D.C. Professor Brown, who headed up the Peace Studies at Manchester College, had been hosting a series of discussions for some months about war, in general. In late January of 1962, he informed us that a "Ban the Bomb" demonstration was being organized. It was scheduled for mid-February, and they expected to attract approximately 25,000 people, the majority of them college students—from across the nation. At the time, it would be the largest demonstration ever to take place in Washington, soon to be dwarfed by Martin Luther King's rally in the summer of that same year.

Manchester College was founded by the Church of the Brethren, one of the three main pacifist churches, along with the Quakers, and the Mennonites. A group of us wanted to go. We asked the President of the College to give us permission to skip classes on Friday, in order to make it to Washington in time for the various marches and speeches on Saturday. He said no, but we went anyway. Six of us squeezed into a 1955 Ford coupe and took turns driving the 10-12 hours needed to get there. We attended services in one of the Negro churches on Friday evening, then slept in sleeping bags on the floor of a Brethren church, before demonstrating in front of the White House on Saturday morning, marching to Arlington Cemetery at midday and then walking back to the Washington Monument in the afternoon to listen to speeches. In late afternoon, we climbed back into the car and drove all night—almost having an accident, as we were all exhausted—arriving back on campus by mid-morning on Sunday. For a country boy like me, it was one of those never-to-be-forgotten experiences. In the end, we thought we had fooled everyone, that is until a picture was published in *Time Magazine* clearly showing one of us carrying a sign that said Manchester College. Luckily, no one ever said anything to any of us.

However, the single most important event was the birth of the Peace Corps in late 1961. The first volunteers were placed in late 1962. While my work schedule and studies left scant time for television and newspapers, it was impossible to ignore the excitement being generated by this new opportunity. I knew immediately that it was something I wanted to do—that, in and of itself, was a first for me. Sometime during the summer of 1963, I went to nearby Ft. Wayne, Indiana, with my then girlfriend Judy, to take the required test to apply to be a Peace Corps Volunteer. We had talked about getting married and serving together, hopefully in Ecuador, where the Church of the Brethren had some ties. I remember little or nothing about the test, except it was long, and it wouldn't be until early in 1964 that I received a response. By then, girlfriend Judy was a thing of the past, but my passion for the Peace Corps remained unchanged. Even though I didn't fully understand what I was getting into, I was extremely excited about starting an adventure that would totally change my life in so many ways.

I grew up during those four years of college. While I still maintained close contact with my family, I was living on my own and making all of my own decisions—some good, some not so good, I'm sure. I was independent in every sense of the word, and suffered some of the hard knocks that occur when somehow making a living, dealing with small crises, interacting with employers, classmates, teachers, and coaches. These demands, though, prepared me for going out to face the rest of the world. Little did I know then what the world had in store for me.

HUBERT R. NEWCOMER, Pastor
506 E. Ninth St. — Phone 401

MISS RUTH GRAHAM
  Director of Christian Education
MARLIN S. BRIGHTBILL
  Minister of Music
R. V. BOLLINGER
  Moderator
CHURCH OFFICES:
  606 North Mill St.
PHONES:
  Church—589
  Offices—139

Manchester Church of the Brethren

SIXTH AND WALNUT
NO. MANCHESTER, IND.

November 14, 1961

Dear Loren:

You have always impressed me as a very fine young man. I noticed you especially as soon as I came here. I appreciate the way you serve as usher, your considerateness in the store when you were clerking. You always walk tall and straight. — I admire that.

I do not know what you are studying. Just what you do is not so important as how you do it and with what attitude. I expect something significant from you. I pray you will find life rich and satisfying as you find your place of work and service. God has need of such as you.

Sincerely your friend,

Ruth Graham

Life-altering letter from Ruth Graham, the Manchester Church of the Brethren's Director of Christian Education.

Finnell, Fessele Elected Managers For 1961-62 O.L.

The Student Publications Committee recently appointed Loren Finnell as the new "Oak Leaves" business manager and Rainer Fessele as the new "Oak Leaves" circulation manager.

Loren, a freshman, is a business major. He is the son of Mr. and Mrs. Ralph Finnell of Chicago, Illinois. Loren stated that it was an honor to receive the job and that he hopes to "attain a working relationship with the editor in putting out a good paper next year." Loren played football this year and participated in high school sports.

Rainer, also a freshman, is a business major. He is the son of Mrs. Elsa Fessele of Cliffside Park, New Jersey. He said that he was "thrilled" when told during biology class that he had received the position. Rainer is an active member of the Young Republicans Club and IRC on campus; he participated in Hi-Y and German Club in high school. He also works as a lab assistant and as a waiter in the dining hall.

Loren Finnell, new O.L. business manager, and Rainer Fessele, new circulation manager, are already working on their proposed budget and method of O.L. distribution for next year. See story on page one.

III

Professional Life

Peace Corps Training

Bozeman, Montana

It was mid-March of 1964. I was still in Kalamazoo, Michigan, working for the accounting firm of Ernst & Ernst, not having heard from the Peace Corps about my application. I was on a three-month internship—part of the college curriculum—and I would most likely get an offer to start work right after graduation. Email, of course, did not yet exist. Picking up the telephone was a costly, major decision, but I felt compelled to do so. The person I spoke to was able to look up my file while I was still on the phone, and my prayers were answered. I had been selected to attend a training session at Montana State College (now Montana State University), starting two weeks after my graduation, with my confirmation and instructions already in the mail.

At that time, only one person in 100 got invited to training. If I successfully completed the training, I would be going to Ecuador—just what I had hoped for. I was ecstatic! I finished my internship in good order. I did get an offer to work for them on a permanent basis, which I politely declined. At least, I hope I was polite. I really have no memory of that.

In mid-June, two weeks after graduating, I climbed into a two-engine prop plane at Chicago's O'Hare Airport and landed in Bozeman, a couple of hours or so later. The country boy from Indiana was about to be taken completely out of his environment.

The adventure had begun, but it was still way too early in my own personal development to have any real idea of what all of this meant. I was starting a career without even a vague picture of where I wanted to end up. None of what I was doing had ever crossed my mind. Other than a one-week class trip to Washington, D.C. and New York during my senior year in high school, and the previously mentioned weekend trip to Washington, D.C., I'd never really been outside of North Manchester, Indiana. I had never interacted with persons from another country or culture, and had paid little or no attention to politics or world affairs. If someone had told me at that time that I was headed into a career that would literally take me around the world a couple of times, make multiple trips to 44 countries on three continents, and interact with high-ranking foreign dignitaries, I would not have believed it. I might not even have wanted to continue. However, had I also been told that it would provide the opportunity to assist millions of persons living in poverty, both directly and indirectly, I probably would have been excited to move forward, and excited is what I definitely was at that moment. I had never been on such an adventure.

Thirty-seven of us from all over the United States assembled in the afternoon of that same day to receive a briefing. With the exception of four or five of us, everyone was in their 20s, and most were recently graduated. We were destined to work alongside agricultural extension workers in rural areas of Ecuador. Montana State College, which offered an agricultural degree, was in charge of the training, and they had subcontracted those responsible for language training and other components. Several persons from Ecuador were invited to Montana to handle the cultural aspects.

The days were extremely intense. We would stumble out of our bunk beds when the bell rang at 6:00 a.m. every day and run bleary-eyed to the football field, where we played soccer or did some other kind of physical exercise for an hour. We then ran back to the quad where we were staying, showered and made our way to the cafeteria for breakfast. The first class in the morning was Spanish, which started at 8:00 am. This was followed by Ecuadorean history, geography, or culture—and then Spanish lab sessions. During lunch, we were told to speak only Spanish or not at all. At 1:00 pm, we had Spanish conversation classes, after which we received some technical instruction in agriculture. Then more Spanish. After dinner, we had assignments to do on our own, or sometimes there were cultural activities such as learning to dance Ecuadorean style and learning the Ecuadoran national anthem. Unlike college, there were no free periods—no time to even think.

We were finished at about 9:00 p.m. each night and usually so mentally and physically tired that we hit the sack right away—that is, until someone found the Hofbrauhaus—about six or so blocks away. After that, the evening schedule included time for a pitcher or two of brew before calling it a day.

In spite of being a teetotaler, I too joined in, as we were being watched all the time, and any anti-social behavior would be frowned on. It was my first taste of beer. North Manchester was a dry town. Moreover, the Brethren, as a rule, did not drink. It was totally prohibited for the college students. I simply had never had the opportunity, so my education in this area was abrupt and sometimes painful.

The schedule of classes and instruction ended at 1:00 p.m. on Saturday, and they packed us off in groups and took us to the countryside. And what a beautiful place it was, full of empty spaces, wooded areas, mountains, lakes, deer, moose, and elk. We climbed Mt. Sacajawea, slid down glaciers on our backsides, went horseback riding, and much more. At night, we would lie in our sleeping bags and gaze at a sky full of stars, totally uninhibited by city lights. On one of those weekends, I woke up with the morning sun to see a full-grown male moose, standing knee deep in a small mountain lake, less than 50 feet away. The weekends were always special, but on Sunday afternoon, we came back to campus and the reality of the training.

It was a beautiful Saturday afternoon, and we were in a respite from the daily grind of Peace Corps training. We were somewhat comfortably situated on a rocky ledge in a wilderness area outside of Bozeman, watching the roaring flow of the river below and the passing wildlife, as well as taking in the breathtaking view of mountainous terrain. Mostly, however, we were just glad not to be in language lab repeating Spanish dialogues we barely understood the meaning of, or rushing off to learn something about the geography and political history of Ecuador. We were free to enjoy what we were going to be doing for the next 36 hours—absolutely nothing.

My new friend, who I was just getting to know, was a 48-year-old, chain smoking, pig farmer from California. As I was a recent college graduate from the Midwest, neither one of us had a real clue about where our adventure was about to take us, and we had scant time to even consider it, given the daily schedule we were being submitted to. Given our age difference, and our dissimilar backgrounds, we were unlikely soul mates, but in fact, we were on a fast track to becoming life-long friends.

Moritz Thomsen, a very liberal thinker in many ways, had been born into a well-known family, whose patriarch was a prominent member of the Republican Party. Moritz was estranged from his father, and having turned his back on the opportunity for wealth and notoriety that would have come along, his life path eventually took him to California where, for some reason, he became a pig farmer. While pursuing this business venture, he also began building a brand new house on the property, eventually failing on both counts. Moritz had such a soft heart that he could not come to terms with the thought of slaughtering the animals he'd cared for on a daily basis. He literally loved them. In the end the pigs were living with him in the unfinished house and he was sleeping with them at night to keep warm. The end result was bankruptcy.

When he later wrote about walking around the table contemplating the Peace Corps application in the first page of his book, *Living Poor*, he really had no other choice. It was either that or live in the streets.

I don't think Moritz ever owned more than two or three pair of torn jeans and some worn-out shirts. At least I never saw him in anything else. And he was never afraid to say whatever was on his mind, things that were sometimes controversial and oft times humorous. He likewise massacred the Spanish language right up to the sad end of his life. Notwithstanding, he was also like a loveable teddy bear, which you wanted to hold and protect. He had no enemies. I think it was those personal qualities that kept him from getting "deselected" during the extremely demanding training that we were subjected to.

Spanish was obviously the single most important part of our training. They had divided us into four groups, based on our ability in Spanish. The A group could speak some Spanish or had taken Spanish in college. Group B, where I landed, had shown some ability to speak during the short exam they gave us on day one. I had taken Spanish in high school. The Cs needed a lot of help, and the Ds much more.

I loved my group in spite of the pressure. My teacher was Cuban. She had just recently escaped from Cuba and couldn't speak any English, so consequently used no English in class. We were taught to speak and think in Spanish—not translate. A mesa was a mesa. It was not table = mesa. We memorized dialogues. We spoke at whatever level we could. We repeated things during lab times and had conversation periods.

The lab periods were almost my downfall. We would repeat things like, Donde estan los alumnos; Los alumnos llegan a la puerta; Como esta la puerta; La puerta esta abierta. That was all fine and good, but they were listening to you. If you made a mistake, they would break in and correct you. That meant that you would catch the next phrase in the middle, making it difficult to repeat, and they would break in again. I usually muddled through, but one day I had more than a bit of trouble and they bounced me from the B group down to the C group. Not only was it humiliating, the teacher in the C group was not that good, and I was no longer learning. Luckily I was able to redouble my efforts and get back to where I felt more comfortable—Group B.

In spite of our struggles, the methods were successful. Dr. Jousti, the European man—I don't remember from where—who was in charge of the language portion of our training—spoke 14 languages, and he had little patience for anyone who couldn't learn just one. Somewhere, midway through the training in Bozeman, he popped into our conversation class after lunch and just stood there listening. One of the women in our group got a bit flustered, couldn't get the words out, and started to cry. He said something simple to her in French, and she replied in English, saying, "I know what you said, but I can't answer." He then said something equally simple to her in Spanish, and she immediately answered in Spanish.

"See," he said, "You had four years of college French, and you can't speak a word. You've had several weeks of Spanish and you can already converse." With that, he turned on his heel and exited.

George Baker, a fellow trainee, recently wrote me about another Dr. Jousti memory: "Que es el cuerpo de paz?" (What is the Peace Corps?) would dictate the rest of my life. His question was directed straight at me, and he stared out of those bright blue eyes. Within the first minute of Spanish training, I froze, having no idea what he said, as I had been put in group A by mistake. Instead of James Baker, who was pulled out of group C that same day when they realized the mistake, Jousti kept me in group A for the challenge of training a "sub primate." Those were probably the best days of my early life, and those experiences would dictate the rest of my life.

We spent 10 weeks in Bozeman. Near the end of the fifth week, we were told that we would be receiving an envelope as we returned from the football field and that it would contain some instructions. All too soon, we found out what that meant. On the fateful morning, we jogged back to the quad as always, only to find our Residential Advisor standing there with a stack of envelopes. Later we would learn that some of the envelopes would contain a message that said: "Congratulations, you have been selected to continue training," while the others said something like "Report immediately to Room X in Y Building."

We never saw any of those people after that. They had been "deselected" and were packed up and shipped off by the time we finished breakfast. The only things we heard were the screams and the crying. There was another deselection process at the end of the ten weeks, and a final one following our time in Mexico.

On the final weekend in Bozeman, we camped out in Yellowstone Park. After that, it was off to Mexico.

The training pushed us all to the limit and made us find a way to go the extra mile, even when we didn't think we could. It made us dig deep within ourselves. For me, at least, I also came away with a new understanding of "learning." In college, we tended to learn things in the sense that we memorized enough facts to enable us to be able to pass the examination. After that, there was little incentive to retain the knowledge for future use, especially in those subjects outside our major area of concentration. In this case, it was much more than just being able to pass the test. Our ability to work and function in Ecuador would depend on how well we could communicate, requiring us to permanently retain and continue building on whatever we were able to absorb during the weeks of training.

Candidates invited to Peace Corps training,
along with instructors and staff,
Roberts Hall, Bozeman, Montana.
June 1964.
From the right: I am standing in back,
directly in front of the first set of double doors, in a white shirt.

Peace Corps Training

Patzcuaro, Mexico

Those of us who survived the second deselection process piled into a chartered two-engine prop plane in Bozeman and headed for the second part of our adventure. We were off to spend August and September of 1964, in Mexico and test our ability to speak Spanish.

I was part of the group that was left off across the Rio Grande from Nogales. The other half proceeded on to El Paso. We already had our instructions. They had given each of us a small amount of money and told us what our destination was. We were told to travel in smaller groups of no more than 5-6, and we had three days to make it to a United Nations Center in Patzcuaro, just south of Guadalajara. They suggested buses as the means of transportation, but did not tell us where to catch them. If we didn't make it in three days, we were automatically deselected.

We formed our little group, crossed the border, found the bus terminal and were soon seated in a Cuatro Estrellas bus heading south. We pretty much lived on that bus for the next 24-36 hours—my memory is foggy here—sleeping on it and eating something wherever it made regular stops. We tried to strike up conversations along the way, and were amazed at the number who'd never heard of the United States and had no idea of where it was. One certainly could not make that statement in today's world.

When we reached Mazatlan, on the west coast of Mexico, we had traveled about three-quarters of the total distance we needed to go, so we decided to splurge on a seaside hotel, take a swim, and sleep in a real bed. It turned out to be another one of those never-to-be-forgotten experiences for me.

I had been a swimmer all of my life, probably since I was five years old. I had experience in swimming pools, small and major lakes, as well as fast-flowing rivers. More importantly, I was physically fit. While I had never been in the ocean, it didn't seem to be a big deal, so I walked right out to where the waves were beginning to break. I tried to dive through one of those waves, but I caught it at its strongest point and it slammed me violently to the bottom. Then the undertow began to drag me out to sea. I had enough presence of mind not to fight it. I waited until its strength lessened and then headed upwards to get some air. I did manage to get a small gulp, but another one of those big waves hit me, again slamming me violently to the bottom. I still did not fight the undertow and waited for my chance to surface. but I was thinking all that time, that I would not be able to withstand a third wave. God must have been watching over me, because I was able to get my head above water and ride the waves back to shore. I crawled up on the beach to contemplate my near-death experience.

We made it to Patzcuaro in good time, as did all of our colleagues, and we settled into a United Nations training facility that was not being used at the time. The first and third weeks were dedicated to learning more Spanish, in the classroom and putting it to use visiting various nearby places. During the second and fourth weeks, we were sent out individually to preselected villages and towns, where we lived with a local family. The girls, and the guys whose Spanish still needed a lot of help, were given some easy assignments. Some of the rest of us were given more challenging places to spend the week—far away from cities and towns. I didn't know this until I reached my destination.

I was ushered into a jeep and the only thing I really knew was that I was going away for a week, and I was expected back at the U.N. Center on such-and-such a day. Since my Spanish was still very elementary, I didn't understand much else. After traveling on a paved road for about 45 minutes, we took off on a dirt road for another 30 minutes—about eight miles—

until we reached a small village where I was let out. There were a handful of adobe homes with an unpaved basketball court in the middle. I was led to a house on the corner, a place that sold an assortment of canned foods, etc, and was told that this was where I had to stay. I had to eat in another house, and all the finances had been taken care of. Then they left without any further instructions.

The only other thing I knew was that I was supposed to blend in and do whatever my hosts were doing. Well, the crops—corn mostly—had already been planted. They didn't need weeding and weren't ready to harvest, so the workers were mostly drinking. There couldn't have been more than 100 people in the village, making it very difficult for a gringo—whom I don't think they had ever seen before—to blend in.

On the first afternoon, we played a lot of basketball, which they liked that because they had never seen anyone as tall as me, and the height of the baskets was such that I could easily dunk the ball. The room they had allotted me was bare, except for the cot, where I placed my sleeping bag. It was fine except for the bed bugs—or similar creatures—that attacked me every night. I had been given some bug spray, however, which saved the day.

The food was very edible, albeit unvaried. When I went to the other house for breakfast, I was served an incredibly great cup of coffee which was made simply by dumping ground-up coffee beans into boiling water. The rest of the breakfast included the best refried beans I've ever had in my life, a fried egg, a banana and tortillas. That menu was the same for lunch and dinner as well—all five or six days I was there.

I somehow made it through the days ahead, but I got physically tired trying to speak Spanish and trying to understand what they were saying. I would often retreat to my room, take a rest from it all, and plan for my return to the U.N. Center, as I had not been paying any attention on the way in. Every day I would ask someone if there was only one road out to the main highway. The answer was always, "Si."

When the day finally came for my return to civilization, I was off at the crack of dawn with my backpack firmly secured. Unfortunately it was raining, but in my own mind, it was a great day. The roads were muddy and slick, but I was making pretty good time and thinking I would reach the paved road soon—that is until I ran into the first fork in the road. As it turned out, there was only one way out—true enough—but there were many different roads. The Gods were with me again, though, and my exit was easy. Once I got to the main road, I flagged a bus and was soon back at the Center.

In many ways, the exit from this Mexican village symbolizes my entire adult life after college. Upon graduation, I could have taken the path that led to being a CPA with a large accounting firm in the Midwest, marriage, a family, comfortable living and friendship with persons I had grown up with. However, had I taken that path, I would not have learned Spanish, and a spattering of other languages. I would not have traveled the world and met so many interesting people with different backgrounds and ways of thinking. I would not have had the opportunity to know what real poverty is, nor would I have had the great satisfaction of lending a helping hand to those same individuals. I thanked God for leading me down the correct road out of that Mexican village, and I thank him every day for helping me choose the correct path in life.

The second trip to the village was a bit more relaxed, as part of the time was spent in a larger town where everyone went to celebrate Mexico's Independence Day.

These two experiences left me with considerable doubt about whether I really wanted to go to Ecuador. I did not believe I would be able to withstand that type of lifestyle for two years. I found out later that I was one of four or five persons who were given the toughest tests to see what we were made of. My living conditions in Ecuador, while not luxurious, were not as severe. Nevertheless, I decided that if I was selected to go to Ecuador, I would make the trip and test the waters before making any final decision.

At the end of our time in Patzcuaro, with its beautiful lake and hand-made crafts, and its friendly people, we were bused to Mexico City in a group and did a day or two of sightseeing before the trip home. During that time, my new-found friend, Moritz Thomsen, was sitting on a bench in one of the parks we visited, where he tried to strike up a conversation with a man who was sitting next to him. According to Moritz, he spent about five minutes or so telling this gentleman, in his best Spanish, who he was and why he was in Mexico. After he'd finished, the gentleman turned to him and politely said, "Siento mucho Señor, yo no hablo Inglés." Moritz somehow found humor in the response. He did go on to Ecuador as a volunteer, and he remained there for the rest of his life, writing several incredible books about his experiences.

Moritz was a fantastic writer. All during our Peace Corps tenure in Ecuador, he sent regular articles to the *San Francisco Chronicle*. They were extremely humorous and poignant, and he later put them together in book called *Living Poor*, unquestionably, in my own mind, the very best book ever written by an ex-volunteer about their Peace Corps experience. Moritz never returned to the U.S., instead moving to Rio Verde, a small village beyond Esmeraldas on the northern coast of Ecuador that could only be accessed by walking along the beach during low tide. There he wrote two more equally incredible books: *The Farm on the River of Emeralds* and *The Saddest Pleasure*, both of which are now out of print and virtually impossible to find. On one of my consultative trips to Ecuador, in August of 1989, I located Moritz in Guayaquil by asking the owner of a bookstore— a contact provided by another former volunteer. I found him in a squalid, two-room walk-up apartment, which he never left due to his advanced emphysema, and he was still smoking. We reminisced for awhile, and then I had to go. Moritz was the epitome of "living poor," and a wonderfully loving and talented person. He was the embodiment of what Kennedy was looking for in a true Peace Corps volunteer. Moritz succumbed to cholera less than two years after my visit. Pat Joseph, a San Francisco-based editor and author visited Moritz soon after I did and wrote: "…his books were grand and valuable and important for the simple reasons that he wrote about important things and chose to live a life stripped down to its essence. He wrote about himself with such honesty, in the end, that just when you thought he had confessed everything, he would open a new vein and bleed some more."

From Mexico City we all flew off to Dallas, where we would have our final deselection process and then go our separate ways for a couple of weeks, prior to traveling to Ecuador. We were all very happy to have completed the training process and were eager to go home to our respective families—following fourteen weeks of intense training. At the same time, we were deeply concerned about the final decision as to who would go to Ecuador and who wouldn't.

As we deplaned in Dallas and entered the terminal, our hearts thumping at a supersonic rate and our palms dripping with sweat, Dr. Dunbar, the head of the training program in Bozeman, with several others, were there to greet us and hand out the dreaded envelopes. We grabbed them, hurried down the corridor a few paces to be alone, and tore them open. My heart sank! My message was to report to Room X in section Y of the airport. That was the type of message that the deselected persons had received before, and I began to prepare myself for the worst. Neither I nor anyone else said anything. We all just moved ahead. I was one of the first to reach the assigned room, and my heart sank even further. My fears were not allayed until more and more of the group filed in. By that time, I figured that they couldn't be deselecting such as large number of us. Dr. Dunbar soon arrived and congratulated us for completing the training successfully. After tears and hugs, we were sworn in and rushed to make our respective flights home. There were 24 of us in the final group, down from the 37 that had started the training, and those 37 were part of a group of 3,700 who had applied. The entire training period was where I began my love affair with the word "persistence."

The prize—after a long period of training.

My Peace Corps I.D.

Peace Corps

Ibarra, Ecuador

September 1964 - June 1966

After two weeks at home, making sure that we had everything we needed for the entire two years—shipping packages in those days was not recommended, as things tended to get "lost" during the custom inspections—we were on an overnight Pan Am flight out of New York to Quito, the capital city of Ecuador, which is nestled high in the Andes mountains at an altitude of 9,800 feet. We arrived in bright sunshine and were greeted by the municipal band and a handful of dignitaries. The band struck up their national anthem, and we proudly demonstrated, loud and clear, that we knew the words.

The first couple of weeks were dedicated to orientation, which included spending some time with one of the volunteers from the first group who were about to return home. I was sent to Alausi, a city in the southern part of the country, and I came back to Quito relieved with the knowledge that the working conditions there were much better than the situation I had faced in Mexico.

Upon returning, we were given our permanent assignments and to my surprise, I would not be working in the agricultural extension program. Given my accounting background, they had selected me to work with a carpentry cooperative another volunteer had founded in Ibarra, which needed some follow-up. Typical of all our Peace Corps experiences to date, we were on our own. They gave me the name of the volunteer and pointed me in the direction of the bus terminal in the southern part of the city, nothing more.

The Pan American highway is now fully paved, but at that time it was a cobblestone road wide enough for about a car and a half. This meant that if you met oncoming traffic, one or both vehicles would have to give ground. Buses obviously did not move a whole lot unless it was another bus, but the scary part of the ride was the terrain. One side of the road was a steep mountainside, the other a precipice falling straight down, hundreds, if not thousands of feet, and the road side was littered with crosses in memory of where one or more persons had lost their lives. The ride, which was incredibly beautiful and passed by at least a couple of snow-covered mountains, took six hours to get to Ibarra. It can now be traversed in one-third that time.

Ibarra, set in another valley of the two chains of the Andes mountains, is at a lower altitude—about 5,500 feet—where the weather is more moderate. It is a provincial capital and the population at the time was about 100,000. Due to its location, the regional office of the Peace Corps was there, and a Regional Director, who oversaw all of the volunteers in the northern part of the country. I found the office very easily by simply asking the first kid I saw, who insisted on carrying my duffle bag, which was bigger than he was. I hung out there for a few days, until I was able to find a more permanent place to live.

The volunteer I was replacing strongly suggested I live alone, rather than with other volunteers—an option I had—as it would force me to utilize my Spanish more. The family that ran one of the many pharmacies in town, one which was located on one of the two main plazas, offered me a couple of rooms in the large two-story building that was their home and encompassed the business. I had running water in my apartment—which I couldn't use for fear of amoebas—and there was a small, out-house type facility—within the confines of the house—just down the hall. Showers, just like out on the farm, were taken once a week—on Friday or Saturday evening—but there were many wood-burning bathhouses nearby where you could get a nice hot shower for a few cents. Given the coolness of the weather, one did not sweat as much. Thank goodness.

This seemed to fulfill all of my basic needs, so I lived there for several months before I noticed an inconvenience. The pharmacist, who was extremely friendly, had several prized fighting cocks that began to show up tethered near my rooms—which had some windows, but no window panes to inhibit noise. Sometime soon after midnight, the cocks would begin to crow, which was very loud and bad enough, but even worse, I found out, that two to three minutes after they crowed, there would be an answer from another rooster several blocks away. However faint it was, it was noticeable, and once the first rooster woke me, I couldn't go back to sleep, waiting the next few minutes for the answer to come. This in turn would invoke another crow from my friends outside my door a few minutes later, and on and on. After any number of sleepless nights, I finally approached my landlord, but only after having to figure out not only how one says rooster in Spanish, but how one conjugates the verb for "crowing"—much more complicated than you would think and difficult to pronounce. Fortunately, the problem was solved after they moved me up to two rooms on the second floor, ones near the area where laundry was done and likely more often used by the maids.

In mid-March 1965, sometime before the move upstairs, I exited from my main-floor apartment, as I normally did every morning on my way to find some breakfast and then go on to work. However, this day was very different. Even before I could close the door, two projectiles of some sort came my way and exploded in wetness on the floor behind me. I immediately returned to my room to survey what had happened and observed the remnants of two balloons beside puddles of water. I slowly stuck out my head to examine the situation further, only to have two more balloons come pummeling down, again narrowly missing me and exploding their contents near my feet. This time I was able to catch a glimpse of two of the young daughters of the pharmacist standing on the balcony and laughing. After considering the situation for a few moments and still not understanding it,

I slammed the door shut and made a mad dash down the corridor to the front door, managing to avoid still other balloons that were tossed my way. I headed directly to the Peace Corps office instead of going my normal route to work. Taking refuge there, I was informed that we were in the last few days before lent and the carnival season had begun. For three days, young people roamed the streets and used various methods of getting anybody and everybody wet. This went on until about 5:00 p.m., after which the private parties, dancing, and drinking would commence. As it turns out, we learned about Ecuador history and politics during Peace Corps training, as well as memorized the names of all of the provinces, their capitals, the mountains and the rivers. We had also learned national anthem and how to dance, but somehow no one had remembered to prepare us for the celebration of carnival.

During the last six months of my tenure, when my Spanish was much better, I moved to a small house with two or three other volunteers, who became my life long friends.

Food was handled in a variety of ways. There were no cooking facilities in the first place I lived, so I made the rounds of restaurants, where you could get something cheap, yet palatable. During the later period, we did some of the cooking until we found a woman willing to do it for us. We had lunch and dinner in her home everyday.

Money was tight, but the amount was tenable. We were given the equivalent of $100 in local currency—Sucres—every month, which had to cover everything. We were not allowed to obtain money from home or any other source. We were convinced that we were "roughing it," and sacrificing—that is until we learned that most of the people we were assisting had to feed their whole families on much less than $100 a month.

My job was challenging, yet interesting. Most carpenters, and there were many of them in Ibarra, worked individually and usually stayed in a room they rented out somewhere. The volunteer that I was replacing had managed to convince about a dozen of them that they could cut their expenses by all working in one place purchasing wood, glue, and paint in larger lots. The idea, of course, was right on, but the implementation much more difficult. Getting twelve people to agree about how things should be done is not that easy. Finding the capital to buy materials in larger lots is even more difficult. Dividing up the work among carpenters, with differing skill levels, was even more complicated. Assisting with all of these factors, when you're just learning about the culture, and when your Spanish is still far from perfect, made it nearly impossible.

In the end, I was able to join forces with John Link, a Papal volunteer from the Catholic Church. He was working with a shoemakers' cooperative, and together we put together a cement-block-making cooperative. We were also able to obtain some donated lands owned by the local Catholic Church in Ibarra, as well as a grant from the Ecuadorean Government, and we oversaw the construction of an Industrial Center for the three cooperatives. While extremely satisfying at the time, and though it may sound like a major accomplishment, the construction of buildings does not guarantee the success of such a project. The cooperatives still needed a lot of assistance and maturation. Soon after we left, all three of them failed—as there was no one to continue with follow up. The only positive outcome was that the buildings are still being utilized for something productive.

There were a million subplots, there. Years later, when I was creating The Resource Foundation, I did so based on the deep belief, that for however well meaning expatriate volunteers may be, it's much more reasonable to allow local people to deal with local problems and limit the expatriate assistance to donated resources.

During my spare time, I taught English at the Ecuadorean-North American Center in the evenings, and raised baby chicks donated by Heifer Project International to give to farmers in the area.

Soon after I began working with the carpenters—the volunteer I was replacing was still there—I had an important learning opportunity. One of the carpenters was getting married, and we were, of course, invited to the wedding. We didn't attend the ceremony, but we did go to the party that followed, held in three rooms of a very modest house in one of the poorer neighborhoods. It had uneven wooden floors, adobe walls, and they had taken out all of the furniture, except for chairs, which were situated side by side around all of the walls. A record player was blaring somewhere and everybody was in their Sunday best—but not suits and ties.

The dancing had not yet started, but one of the guests was going around the room, from person to person, serving a shot of aguadiente, a high-proof liquor somewhat akin to the white lightening produced in Appalachian stills. This person had only one shot glass, which he would fill and then wait until you said Salud (to your health), and drank it down in one gulp. Having only recently learned to drink a glass of beer, this was a bit more challenging for me. However, being a college graduate and a very smart gringo, I came up with a perfect plan to ease this assault on my body. I had noticed that the person doing the serving was not drinking, so somehow I got the bottle and shot glass in my possession and proceeded to make the rounds. Very soon, however, there was a change in the game plan. Each person I served started saying, Usted primero (you first), and instead of only having to drink a shot every 10-15 minutes, I was soon doing one every minute or so. The gringo had been outsmarted, so I ditched the bottle and the shot glass as quickly as possible.

My gringo friend was not a drinker either, so we excused ourselves at the first possible moment. However, they let us go only on the promise that we would come back the next day. Parties of this nature could easily last two or three days.

And go back we did, but only after having a hearty lunch and waiting until about 3:00 pm, thinking they would surely have finished lunch by then. Wrong again! We got there just in time, and we were escorted to the place of honor at the table, where a large bowl of heavy, but very good, soup was set before us. I finished that off, and hoped that whatever came next would be a bit lighter. The next course was a large portion of potatoes along with chicken that had been pulled off the bone. I somehow managed to get that eaten, and I was looking forward to a small desert of some kind, when they brought in what was really the main course—a huge mound of rice with a roasted cuy (guinea pig) on top—head and all, with its eyes staring right at me. How I got that consumed, I have no idea, especially since I didn't know that guinea pig was a food. I thought it was a pet.

However, it wasn't until a lot later that I learned the lesson that I should have learned right then. In the States, at least where I came from in the Midwest, the polite thing to do is to eat everything placed in front of you. It shows your host and hostess, that you appreciate and like what they served you. In Ecuador, the polite thing to do is to leave la politica (a small portion of the food) to show that you have eaten your fill. It took me several similar situations until that custom became embedded in my brain.

The social life was full as well. We used every opportunity possible to have a party of some kind, many of them in the regional offices of the Peace Corps. In addition to the volunteers that worked in and around Ibarra, there were any number who would come in from the countryside for a little R & R. There was also a group of Ecuadoreans our age, who wanted to join in on the fun. That was how I met Pilar. She was the Social Secretary for the Mayor of Ibarra and was introduced to all of the volunteers when they arrived. We didn't start dating until sometime during the second year of my tour. Another Gringo had her eye—until I moved in on his territory.

Soon after I arrived in country, I was set up with a girl who was referred to as la chaparita, due to her small stature. They used to joke about her saying that she wasn't tall enough to besar mi pupo (kiss my belly button). I wasn't particularly attracted to her, but she was someone to pass the time with. The moment came, however, when I knew it was time to call a halt to things. She, and about four or five others, were in the English class I taught one evening a week. For some reason the entire group was walking down the street together when out of the blue she looked at me and said in a loud voice, "Te quiero." Now to me the verb querer meant "to want," as in I want a coke, I want to go somewhere. So I thought to myself, she may want me, but she can't have me, so I just ignored the comment. It wasn't until sometime later that I learned that te quiero more often means "I love you," but even before that happened, I had stopped seeing her socially.

My relationship with Pilar began to flower—literally—around Valentine's Day 1966, when I stole a white rose from the garden in back of the Peace Corps office and gave it to her. Our times together became frequent and were highlighted by a day of mountain climbing, with another couple, to the top of Imbabura—a 15,000 ft. mountain overlooking Ibarra—just before my vacation.

When Regional Director Tom Torres completed his tenure and was leaving the country in September of 1965 to be married in Mexico, he invited me to accompany him for a few days to Bogota and Cartagena, Colombia, to revisit some of places he knew as a volunteer in the very first Peace Corps group to serve anywhere—though the Ethiopia Peace Corps was the first group to start the training process. Six months later, I still had some vacation time left so Curt Larson, Gary Gabriel, and I decided to head south for a month.

It would be considered as a very exciting trip for most anyone—even today—but it was particularly so for neophytes like us. And since travel to Latin America was not as common then, as it is now, I remember writing home to my folks telling them that this adventure was only going to cost us $500 for everything.

It was mid February 1966, when we flew to Lima, Peru, and stayed with Tom Torres and his wife Diane for a few days. Tom had become the Peace Corps Director, there. Then it was on to Cuzco—in a two-engine prop plane that had no air pressure system. Since Cuzco itself is more than 10,000 feet high, we needed to suck oxygen from a plastic tube and put cotton in our ears as we weaved back and forth up the river valleys, prior to landing on a muddy, unpaved runway. One month after we returned to Ecuador, this same airplane crashed into the side of the mountain, killing all aboard, including a Peace Corps volunteer from Peru.

After making the rounds of Cuzco, with its incredible Incan stonework topped by fabulously hand-carved wooden verandas, we purchased alpaca sweaters, and took the 5:00 a.m. train to visit Machu Picchu. What a fabulous place! Making a lunch out of canned tuna, we perched on a hilltop overlooking the magnificent ruins.

The next morning we left for Lake Titicaca on an ancient, coal-burning train. We sat across from a British mother and son, who were breakfasting on gin and tonics. After boating out to visit some of the floating islands, and doing some other sightseeing, we were able to negotiate a private car at a good price to take us all the way down to the coast and on to the border with Chile.

What a stark difference to be in the dry, arid coast after spending days in the snow-covered Andes Mountains. We crossed the border into Chile and then continued by bus, making a brief stop in the mining capital, Antofagasa, before continuing on to Santiago—a nonstop trip of 27 hours, —sitting in a cramped space not meant for gringo types.

After several days enjoying the beautiful capital city, its delicious food, and world-famous wines, we took a small bus up and over part of the skiing area of Chile, and down into Mendosa, Argentina, where we stayed long enough to taste some of their equally famous wines.

From there we were able to find an extremely comfortable bus, with food service and a restroom. It took us across the entire country to Buenos Aires, the "New York" of Latin America. What a difference from the indigenous cultures we had been used to in Ecuador and Peru! Armed with a brief educational tour, we flew back to Lima, and then on to Quito, taking along with us the memories of our first good look at a wide range of differences in the sub-cultures that exist in South America.

I received some unwelcome news upon my return. Even before I got back to Ibarra, several volunteers in Quito informed me that there was a new Regional Director in Ibarra, and that he was "hitting" on Pilar. Needless to say, I took the next bus out and returned to protect my territory. Thank goodness the stories were exaggerated.

That good fortune was soon overshadowed by some bad news. Within two weeks after we returned to Ecuador from our vacation, Curt "Tony"

Larson was killed, along with several other people, in an accident when the vehicle they were riding in went off the road and crashed in a deep ravine.

It fell on Todd Tibbals, the new Regional Director—and now life-long friend—to deal with this situation. He recently wrote me about Tony's passing, "The day Tony died, I was talking to Galo Plaza (former President of Ecuador) about his request for two volunteers to work with the indigenous groups living at his hacienda Zuleta. His secretary answered the phone and then approached us, saying that Curt Larson had died. Gary Gabriel and I took my Jeep Wagoneer to El Angel, getting there after dark. Hundreds of locals were paying tribute to Tony's coffin, while hardly noticing the three dead Ecuadoreans. We had to bribe the Transit Judge to get the body released, but he wouldn't give us any paperwork. Around midnight, while en route to Quito, we got mired in mud in a Paramo downpour. Our humor waxed sick as we asked Tony's permission to remove him from the jeep during this episode, which finally ended about 2:00 a.m. Arriving at the checkpoint (for Colombia contraband) just north of Ibarra, the bleary-eyed guard waved us through, commenting to his compañero, that 'the gringos are now smuggling Colombian coffee in coffins.' The remainder of the trip to Quito was uneventful."

Soon after, the Industrial Center I had been working on was inaugurated at a ceremony attended by the American Ambassador. A week later Pilar flew off to Dallas with Linda Smith, a volunteer who had completed her tour. The two of them planned to visit the Midwest and the Boston area. Pilar and I had made plans to meet as soon as I mustered out of the Peace Corps when I'd completed my tour in Ecuador a few weeks later.

I matured during these two years. It was the first time in my life that I had to deal with the death of someone so close, who wasn't a grandparent, and there were a lot of other firsts as well. I began to learn how to outwardly express my feelings—something we didn't do at home. We were not "huggers" in spite of caring very strongly for one another. In Ecuador, "abrazos" were commonplace among friends, even among male friends, and walking along arm-in-arm was also an accepted practice. There were any number of other customs which I found beneficial to acknowledge and accept.

Having grown up in a very conservative Protestant community, I was suddenly thrust into a society where nearly everyone was Catholic and where the churches were ornate and the services ceremonial—filled with ritual. This, too, I learned to take in stride.

Most of all, I had to come face to face and deal with a level of poverty that far outstripped even the very difficult times my own family had experienced. This impacted me deeply. It made me more committed than ever about what I wanted to do with the rest of my life. I had found my calling.

Carpenter Cooperative Marching in Pro Government Rally,
Ibarra, Ecuador.

Rabbit hutch I built for a family
receiving rabbits from the Heifer Project.

Laying the cornerstone for Industrial Park.
The Bishop and the Mayor of Ibarra (center).

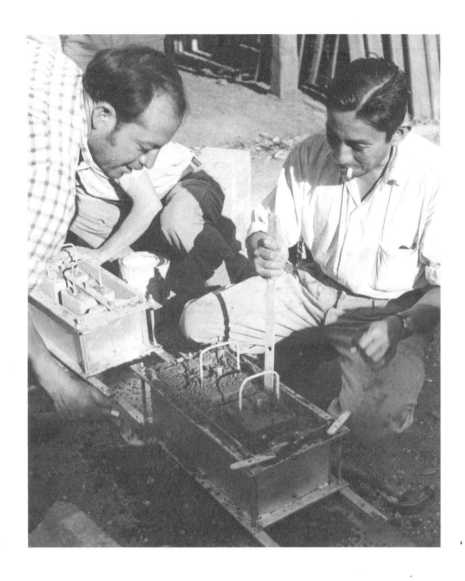

Some of the carpenters
making cement blocks for the new construction.

Here I am, with another volunteer, helping in the construction.

Shovel in hand, I am helping clear debris
in front of the nearly completed Artisan Park project.

The three buildings of Artisan Park from a distance.

Here, I'm receiving an award at the opening ceremony,
attended by the Provincial Governor and the U.S. Ambassador
(seated far left, respectively).

Pilar, and "you know who,"
in front of the completed Industrial Artisan Park.

International Voluntary Services (IVS)

Vientianne, Laos

September 1966 -September 1968

By the time I returned to my parents home in Chicago in late June, Pilar had already been to Boston and back by car, and was learning what a hot and humid summer was like in Dallas. We soon organized a mini-re-union at Linda Smith's home that included three other Ecuadoreans who were visiting in Kansas, as well as former Peace Corps volunteers Gilberto Lopez from Arizona and Gary Gabriel from Minnesota.

Soon after, Pilar traveled by train to Chicago. During her visit, I learned that the Peace Corps was not only offering me a job at a training site in Puerto Rico, but that Pilar would have a job as well. What great news, but since there was very little time, we had to plan our wedding in the suburbs of Chicago instead of returning to Ecuador. This caused a few rumbles, but we finally received the blessings of Pilar's father, and the wedding was on. Fortunately, we were able to get the same group together that had been in Dallas. Pilar got her own bedroom on the night before the big event, and the rest of us were spread out on the living room floor.

Two very close friends of my folks also attended the affair, along with my sister, her two children, an aunt, two cousins and my grandmother Hart-sough—a guest list of 16. The "after" party was held at my folks' home with homemade sandwiches, macaroni salad, and cake for all. Also on the menu was champagne—an inclusion that caused our first argument. The

64

champagne was a gift from my best man, Gilberto. I told Pilar that since my grandma was there, we couldn't serve it. I not only lost that argument, Pilar served grandma two glasses of the bubbly brew, and she loved it.

Since Gilberto, Gary and the three Ecuadoreans friends had come from such a distance, we couldn't just go off on our honeymoon and leave them, so we all went to the Playboy Club in downtown Chicago for dinner and then on to an evening of dancing before heading off on our own to a cottage on Rock River that my folks co-owned with another couple. This was the first time Pilar and I had ever been alone together, as dates in Ecuador had always been group affairs.

So there we were, united and ready to face the world. I was a Protestant, reserved, a time freak, a tosser, and a country boy. Pilar was a Catholic, outgoing, always late, a saver and into the arts. And then there were the language and culture issues. No one thought we had a chance to make it, but here we are 45 years later and still married.

After returning from the honeymoon, we decided to travel to Boston to be with my sister and brother-in-law for a few days before going on to our new jobs. However, soon after arriving, I received a phone call from the Peace Corps indicating that they had to close one of the two training facilities in Puerto Rico. Unfortunately, it was the one where we were to work.

We ended up spending a month at my sister's home, and since we literally were out of money, I spent the entire time working at a nearby McDonalds. During that time, a Brethren friend from North Manchester let me know about a job opportunity with International Voluntary Services (IVS), a nonprofit agency incorporated in the late 1950s that had been a model for developing the Peace Corps. They had a staff opening for an Administrative person in Vientianne, Laos, where they had 120 volunteers on the ground from various countries. The majority were Americans. They were also operational in Viet Nam, where there were another 180 volunteers. After looking at the map to see where Laos was, we decided to do it, in spite of the fact that there was a war raging in nearby Viet Nam. Until we got there, we didn't know that there was a secret war also taking place in Laos.

So off we went to Washington, D.C., and then to nearby Harper's Ferry for a week of orientation—with no language training—before taking a Northwest flight to Tokyo, with stops in Cleveland, Chicago, and Anchorage, arriving in the evening of the same day—after a 19-hour flight. It was a Tokyo much different than what you would find today. There was very little English spoken, no English on signs, and tourism was not a major industry. My feet hung over the end of the hotel bed by more than a foot, and there were 40-watt light bulbs in the lamps.

Be that as it may, we enjoyed a few sights for a couple of days before flying on to Hong Kong, which was much more accustomed to having foreigners. We made the usual visits during our few days there, including a wonderful lunch on a Sampan. Then it was on to Bangkok, Thailand.

Bangkok was scheduled to be a four-hour layover before continuing on to Laos. We were given a chit for lunch in the airport, which we took advantage of, and while watching some of the planes take off and land, I told Pilar I thought I would go to the Air Lao desk and double-check our flight. I told her to wait for me in the main terminal.

I found the Air Lao desk down at the end of a long hall and took my place in line. The gentleman in front of me was an American who asked how long I had been waiting to get on a flight to Vientianne. I indicated that my wife and I had just flown in from Hong Kong, and that we were scheduled to go out in a short time. He laughed and said it wouldn't happen, indicating that they were always overbooked and that he'd been in Bangkok for three days. I panicked! I had a 20 dollar bill in my pocket, no credit cards, and no contacts in Thailand.

Nevertheless, I waited quietly until it was my turn in line and presented my tickets. Sure enough, I was informed that the flight was full and I would have to come back another day. No amount of explaining that we were in transit and our luggage was being loaded on their plane seemed to make any difference. But since persistence was continuing to become my favorite word, I pressed on and got even more insistent.

A few minutes later, they finally said O.K. They had identified one seat and wanted to know if I or my wife was going to fly. I responded with, "No deal. We are both going to fly." Since I didn't budge, they gave the seat to the next person in line.

The desperation made the ugly America come out in me, so I went behind the counter and into the other room, continuing to insist in a very loud voice. After a few more minutes of this, they talked among themselves, and again said O.K. but that we would have to hurry, as the flight was about to leave. They put me in a golf cart, rushed me down to the main terminal to find a very distraught Pilar. I asked her to just be quiet and get on the cart. We were rushed out to the plane, where we boarded and found two empty seats in the back.

The one-hour flight was uneventful, other than trying to explain to Pilar what had happened during the hour I had been absent. However, when we arrived, we had another problem, one that would repeat itself several times during our stay in that part of the world. The customs people in Laos had never heard of Ecuador and said that Pilar needed a visa, insisting that they could not allow her to enter the country. After finally convincing them to talk to the IVS representatives we knew would be waiting for us—and who almost left thinking we did not make the flight—the problem was solved. What a day! And what a welcome to Laos.

IVS had two contracts with USAID (United States Agency for International Development). One was for a rural development team, which was the larger of the two, and the other for education. Each had their own Chief of Party and separate staffs. I was hired as part of what was to be an effort to begin unifying the two. The education team had no administration person, but I was replacing a person on the rural development team who had been there for seven or eight years. As Associate Chief of Party, I was hired to handle all of the administrative duties for both contracts, and I was the communication link between them.

After settling in, Pilar began spending a good deal of time as a non-paid volunteer at the orphanage where two IVS volunteers were working. We would have brought home a Lao child to the States had not the local laws prohibited it.

Neither of us knew any Lao, and we had only a very limited under-standing of French, the second official language. However, over the period of two years, Pilar not only perfected her English by speaking with the IVS staff and volunteers, she also picked up a decent amount of Lao and French as well. My own work situation only allowed me to say enough in Lao to greet people and say, "Thank you." This was probably better, as Lao is a tonal language, with wide-ranging meanings for the same word, depending on how it is pronounced, and I've had a hearing problem all of my life. For example, Pilar once asked the cleaning lady to help serve one evening, telling her that we were going to have some "pigs" over for dinner, instead of "friends." This was cause for a good laugh.

Most of the volunteers with the Education Team were working at Dong Dok, a glorified high school referred to as a university. Most of the students were taught in Lao and some in French. The IVS volunteers obviously han-dled the English. It was a fairly new facility, and thanks to USAID, situated some distance outside of Vientianne. The school was referred to as K9 (Kilometer 9). A complex of two-story apartment buildings had been built for the faculty, and it was there that we found lodging. USAID also pro-vided a small van that made regular trips back and forth to the USAID com-pound in Vietianne, but one could get from place to place in the city via "samlos," a three-wheeled bicycle with space for two passengers behind the bike rider. We also bought a 125cc motorbike, and I had a jeep at my disposal for work-related activity.

In addition to offices, the USAID compound had a dining facility, a swimming pool, and a PX where we could purchase canned food, paper products, and all the rest, as well as meat shipped in from Australia. Shop-ping could also be done at the outdoor Morning Market, where you would find textiles, fresh fruits, vegetables, live frogs, betel nut, opium, heroin, marijuana, or whatever else you wanted. All were legal.

The first time Pilar visited the market and saw the women with the red saliva dripping out of the sides of their mouths as a result of chewing betel nut, she left immediately and came running to my office to be consoled. She thought they had been eating the live frogs.

We soon got to know all the volunteers especially well since we were living so close to the Education Team. The rapport was good as we were young enough to relate and understand them, and we were easily accessible and willing to listen. Since we were staff, they also saw us as people who could do something about their concerns and problems. The proximity of our living quarters provided opportunities for many get-togethers, and our apartment was a favorite gathering spot.

My days were split between the two offices in the beginning, but then in the spirit of trying to unify the two teams, I began to encourage the education volunteers to come to the larger office in Vientianne. I had a staff of six to eight Lao employees to assist me. My basic job was to make sure that the volunteers had everything they needed for their work and for their living quarters. I did all the purchasing and coordinated all the transportation, basically making sure the organizational motor was running smoothly. I was also responsible for keeping track of the volunteers and for their security.

Given the fact that a "secret" war was going on in Laos, and that a good number of volunteers were living in rural areas, it was extremely important to know where everyone was at all times. The ones in Vientianne were fairly easy to track, but those living throughout the country were obligated to call me by radio and let me know the exact hour when they were leaving their post. I had a radio on 100% of the time in the office, and another one in our apartment. Upon arriving in Vientianne, they were required to report to me before doing anything else. If they were overdue by more than 60 to 90 minutes, I was to notify the office responsible for sending out a helicopter search—something I had to do more than once.

The Lao Air Force had a fleet of WWII T-28 planes that went out to bomb the Ho Chi Mein Trail twice a day, and their throaty engines could be heard for a long distance as they took off and returned from duty. On occasion we could hear the thud of the bombs exploding in the distance.

Though Laos was a neutral country, the secret war was more or less common knowledge to citizens in the United States. Much less known, until late in the Vietnam War, was the large air base in the Plane de Jars, in the northern part of the country, where many marines were illegally based, and where air strikes were launched using modern jet planes. It was run by a former Indiana farmer by the name of "Pop" Buell, a fact we were not allowed to talk about, let alone write home about it.

One of the volunteers, who was living in what they called a "forward area," close to the action, was in a plane that was forced to land there due to weather conditions. When he later came to the office to report in with me, he said, "Oh my gosh, you wouldn't believe what I saw." When I asked him to share, he would only repeat his amazement and say that he had been sworn to secrecy. No amount of cajoling on my part could get him to divulge anything.

Much, much more could be said about the secret war and how it affected our lives, but suffice to say that during my tenure, two of my colleagues on the staff were killed, as were four volunteers and two Lao assistants. All of these losses were hard to take, but the one I remember most was related to a volunteer I visited near Pakse in the southern part of the country. He was a new volunteer, so I was there to check out his living and working conditions. He took me out to one of the communities where he was involved, which we reached by driving across the dry rice paddies. He made his visit, and we then sat around drinking a potent local liquor—lao-lao, before we left. On the way out, he told me it was a Pathet-Lao village. In other words, one that was sympathetic to the communist forces. I highly recommended that he not return there, but I guess I didn't get through to him. A short time later, he was shot and killed in that same village.

Somewhere during the later part of our first year in Laos, I experienced a very significant and potentially life-changing event, which related back to the time Pilar and I were at my sister's home in Boston. While there, I had received notice from the Selective Service to report for a physical—which I did. However, my records did not get forwarded from Indiana in time, so the physical did not take place. Unbeknownst to me, when the records did arrive, I had already left for Laos and, since I did not present myself, I was immediately placed on a black list and required to report for duty. Being a member of a pacifist church, I had the option of registering as a conscientious objector—which I am—when I turned 18. Lacking anyone to counsel me, I took the easy way out and ignored it. Besides, there was no war going on at that time.

I was totally unaware that IVS Washington was dealing with the problem. Given the means of communication in the 1960s, I received two missives one day, which I opened. The first one was an air-mail letter from the Selective Service System in Wabash, Indiana, informing me that since I was delinquent, I was to report immediately to Clark Air Force in the Philippines—and that my induction into the Army could not be appealed. I was distraught, until I opened the second envelope. It contained a telegram simply stating that my appeal related to my induction had received a favorable determination by the Presidential Review Board by a vote of two to one—nothing more. After rereading it several times to make sure I understood correctly, there were shouts of joy and a few beers to celebrate.

It's hard to say what would have happened had I not received the favorable vote. More likely than not, I would have ended up in Canada until years later when the United States Government decided to forgive those who fled there to avoid the draft.

In spite of the conflict that surrounded us during our tenure in Laos, we had a tremendous experience. The Lao people were beautiful and very peaceful. They had a simple life and enjoyed it. While we would consider their general condition to be one of poverty, in reality they had few needs. For the most part they had adequate shelter and sufficient food. Education and health services were, however, in short supply.

Once we had gotten used to the 110-120 degree—and above—temperatures and the humidity, we didn't mind it. In fact, when the thermometer dipped into the 90s, we would put on a sweater. The landscape was breathtaking, displaying an abundance of plants and animals. We had a hanging orchid garden in front of our apartment with more than 100 varieties, some of which we helped gather in the forest.

The small lizards that cohabited our home helped us deal with insects and, as long as we kept all the food in the refrigerator, the ants didn't invade us. Even the large green geckos were harmless, but one did manage to give Pilar a scare when it showed up less than a foot away from her face while she was putting on her makeup in the bathroom.

The snakes, both large and small, were to be taken seriously. While tending the orchids one morning, I failed to see a small snake, referred as the "two step," for if bitten, you would likely die within that time period. Someone else did see it and yelled out to me in time. I also remember coming back to K9 on my motorbike one night, when I abruptly came upon a large snake that was crossing the road. I could see neither the head nor the tail, and there was nothing I could do but continue to ride right over it. I had no witnesses, however, and no one ever believed my story.

Pilar and I also had an opportunity to do some traveling, thanks to the fact that some of it was provided free of charge. Air America, a USAID CIA-contracted group—there was a movie made about them—had service to all of the major population centers in the country, as well as trips to Bangkok for medical and dental treatment. We made any number of trips to Bangkok to visit the temples, the floating market, and other sites. We also went there to get some R&R. And Pilar went with a friend to see Luang Prabang, the royal capital of Laos, and on another occasion, when there was a plane that needed to travel to Hong Kong for a routine maintenance checkup she went along for some shopping. This latter trip included a several hour stopover in Da-nang, Viet Nam, the largest American air base and, at that time, the busiest airport in the world, due to the take offs and landings of airplanes going on bombing missions. It was a stopover that left a vivid memory of the war indelibly etched in her mind.

I have my own memory of a flight on Air America—well-known for their eccentric and unorthodox pilots. One took place on a return trip from Bangkok. As we were gaining altitude after taking off from the airport, a loud explosion was heard coming from the right engine. Nobody said a word, and soon thereafter, a second explosion took place. Again, no one said anything, and within a minute or two, the ashen-faced co-pilot came into the cargo area where we were and announced that we would be returning to the Bangkok airport—nothing more. We landed without any further incident, and while we waited on the plane for the repairs to be made, the woman sitting beside me said she had been on that same plane the previous morning, when it flew from Vientianne to Bangkok. She indicated that they'd had difficulty starting the right engine, and that the pilot had exited through an emergency door directly onto the wing, where he had proceeded to kick the engine. He then returned to the cockpit and attempted to start the engine again. It started immediately, and they took off. After I heard that story, I wasn't sure I wanted to continue with the flight, but before I could do anything, we were on our way and returned to Laos without further incident.

On our own, we visited Chiang Mai in the northern part of Thailand, where there is a well-known Buddhist temple. On another occasion, we took some vacation time in Penang, a lovely island off the coast of Malaysia. I too had a side trip during the second year of our stay, when I was asked to spend a month in the Philippines to accompany four new volunteers receiving training at the International Rice Research Institute (IRRI).

For recreation, there was usually a Sunday softball game at the K6 compound, where the majority of the USAID workers lived, and sometimes we challenged the Japanese at their own version of softball. There was also a basketball and a volleyball league. I participated on the IVS teams for both. We regularly beat everyone in basketball, especially the Lao team that was so short in stature. Though when it came to volleyball, we were totally outclassed by them.

We had a very wide range of friends, thanks to Pilar's outgoing personality. The *official* neutral status of Laos and the war in next-door Vietnam resulted in a large number of countries being represented in this small country. Pilar had not only managed to find every person of Latin descent, but we regularly got together with acquaintances from England, Ireland, France, and Israel.

One of the most memorable events took place shortly before our trip home. An Israeli couple we knew invited us to, of all things, a pig roast. There was a large crowd of people invited, representing at least a dozen or more countries. At the end of the evening, we gathered around a blazing fire and, in spite of the heat, began to sing songs in each of the languages represented. It was much fun and left an indelible memory. We also visited two of the Israeli couples, who were present, on our way home.

The time in Laos had certainly widened my perspectives, and it began to hone my management skills and my ability to work with a plethora of different situations and personalities. The experience also convinced me that I was out of my element. I had been offered the option to continue in Laos, or the opportunity to start a new program in Morocco as the Chief of Party. I declined both knowing my knowledge of Latin America and my language skills were better suited, there. Pilar and I headed home, much enriched and with no apprehension about identifying the next challenge.

Pilar, me, and the Priest—to prove to Pilar's father
that we were married in a Catholic Church.
Wheaton, Illinois, August 6,1966.

My dad, mother, Pilar, and me.

In the receiving line at the back of the church.
Wheaton, Illinois, August 6, 1966.

Cutting the cake at home.
Mom, my sister Anne, me, Pilar, Dad—holding my niece Kathy, and
Noemi, a friend from Ecuador.

Doing my administrative duties.

Pilar with some of the volunteers.

Pilar visiting one of the Buddhist temples.

Pilar "Pily" Finnell vacationing in Malaysia
Fall 1966.

Relaxing on the beach in Malaysia.

The Trip Home

October-November 1968

IVS had purchased our return ticket home, and we had saved up $2,000 over the two years. We made up an itinerary that included nine countries and committed ourselves to two months of travel, or as much as we could do without running out of money—whichever came first. Thanks to having a copy of the book *Europe on $10 a Day* and some careful budgeting, the two months and the $2,000 ended in a dead heat.

We left Laos with some sadness, but energized by the expectations of reuniting with friends and family following a lengthy absence. After an overnight in Bangkok, we arrived in our first destination, Cambodia, a country very similar to Laos in terms of ethnic makeup, language, religion, climate, economics, governmental structure, and demeanor of the populace. Given their apparent peaceful nature, it's extremely difficult for us to imagine how the more recent events of genocide took place in those surroundings.

We had one principal reason for making this stop, and that was to follow the recent footsteps of Jacqueline Kennedy visiting the magnificent ancient temple of Ankor Wat. Like Vientianne, Phnom Phen lacked much in the way of structure, so it wasn't too difficult to locate the one service that could take us where we wanted to go. Very early in the morning, Pilar and I, along with about eight others, stuffed ourselves into a Peugeot station wagon, with the baggage on top of the car. It was quite a trip, with Pilar sitting on my lap for eight hours while traveling at 80 miles an hour down a paved road about a car and a half wide, with lots of traffic both motorized and pedestrian.

We spent a couple of days taking in the wonders of Ankor Wat, which is spread over thousands of acres of jungle and some open spaces. Words are totally inaccurate to describe the elaborate carved stone structures and the overlap of trees and other plants. *National Geographic* had a magnificent piece about it a number of years ago. If you can't make a personal visit, it would be worth the effort to search for the article.

We then retraced our steps to Phnom Phen and Bangkok before continuing on to our second stop—New Delhi. It was an Asian culture and situation much different from what we had experienced during the prior two years. India was much more heavily populated. The poverty was many times more acute, the caste system, at least at that time, was difficult to accept and the religious mix was complex.

Here again, we had one basic mission, and after almost losing our suitcases on the flight from Bangkok, we were on our way by bus to Agra to see the Taj Mahal, an incredible edifice that one has to see firsthand to believe. Pilar was particularly struck by its beauty. In spite of not being known as an early riser, she got up at 4:00 am on the second day to see it in the light of the rising sun and take more pictures.

Our next stop, Israel, was the single most important place we visited. We took more than a week to do all we wanted to do. We arrived shortly after the Six-Day War, finding the country abuzz with excitement. This was particularly apparent to us as we spent time with two different couples who had been our friends in Laos—both of whom were heavily involved in politics.

The first couple lived in Tel Aviv. We particularly remember an evening when they took us out to dinner and asked if we liked white steaks. Without knowing what they were, we answered that we liked everything. It turns out that it was a restaurant that featured fire-broiled, extra thick pork chops that were served rare to medium rare. For obvious reasons, they were referred to as "white steaks." They were delicious!

We then went north to Haifa to visit the second couple, who among other things, took us as far as the border with Lebanon, where we got to see a kibbutz firsthand. We were invited to stay there for a month and almost took them up on the offer, but the desire to get back to family and friends made us decline.

The most emotional part of being in Israel, however, was the opportunity to see the religious sites in Jerusalem, Bethlehem, Nazareth and to pass by the Dead Sea. We made these visits by bus, and the one thing Pilar and I both took away from this experience, and could agree on, was just how different everything was from the mental images we had developed over the years from reading the Bible. It was an extremely moving experience, one that reflected Israel's early history.

We had decided to include Turkey in our travel plans, in large part due to the reputation it had for suede clothing and the fact that it could be hand-tailored in a very short time. Among other things, Pilar got a very nice suit made of tan suede and a gray, full-length coat. I got a brown jacket that I still have today. When we tried on the final products, the tailor took the occasion to run his hands all over Pilar, and I mean all over, "to make sure the fit was a good one." For some reason, he did not bother to do the same with me.

The rest of our time in Turkey was filled going to the "thief's" market, the Blue Mosque, and St. Sofia's Cathedral before moving on to Greece, where we enjoyed the Acropolis, the great food, the people, and a boat ride to several of the islands a couple of hours away from Athens.

The second most important portion of our trip was Italy. A week was not nearly enough time to do it justice. Although not being a Catholic at the time—I converted years later in order to be in sync with the rest of my family—I was amazed at the size and grandeur of St. Peter's Basilica and the beauty of the statues and the mosaics. And if *I* was taken by all of this, I can only imagine the importance to Pilar. However it was the tour of the Sistine Chapel that impressed me more than anything. We entered with a group of 15-20 persons, only to find as many as 10 or more other tour groups, each with their own guide explaining all of the important details to be seen in a loud voice and creating quite a din. The woman who was our guide sat us down on some steps and began to describe the Chapel with such emotion that I was easily reduced to tears in spite of the background noise of the other groups and the general confusion. She was able to make us feel that we were part of the history surrounding us, thereby blocking out all of the other distractions. There were many other churches and sculptures to see, as well as the catacombs, the Shroud of Turin and, of course, the Coliseum.

We could not leave Rome without tossing some coins into the Trevi Fountain, so near the end of our time in Italy, we took care of that and then found a nice cozy restaurant nearby where we both ordered lasagna, a salad, and a wonderful red wine. It was so delicious that when the waiter came to ask if we wanted some desert, we just looked at one another without saying anything—and ordered a second round of the same. We must have been hungry, as I don't remember having to force down the second dinner.

And then there was Madrid, with flamenco, paella, rioja wine, the Prado, and a side trip to Toledo to see the art work of El Greco. I thought of my father, wondering how he, who had dinner no later than 5:00 p.m. each night, would have fared in a country where dinner was usually served at 10-11:00 p.m. Except for the difficulty we had understanding the Castilian Spanish—just kidding—we had a wonderful time.

Ooh la la! Paris, and an opportunity for Pilar to practice some French and a chance to see and dance with Can-Can dancers, visit a striptease parlor, and end the evening at the Moulin Rouge, all part of a guided bus tour, which ended with the guide explaining to us in French, English, and German, what the suggested tips were for her and the bus driver. When the bus stopped to let off, several tourists ignored the invitation to give a tip, and the tour guide chased them down and demanded they pay. In view of the fact that I thought the cost of the evening was a bit excessive, and that telling me how much to tip was a bit rude, as well as the fact that we were near the end of our trip and running out of money, I decided on a plan. Noticing that she did not make the announcement in Spanish, I quickly whispered to Pilar and we left the bus near our hotel repeating, "Muchas gracias," over and over. She did not follow us.

We saw the Eiffel Tower, and the other places we didn't want to miss in Paris, and then moved on to London. We spent some quality time with a few friends we had been with in Laos and who were living in a lovely thatched home in a nearby rural area. We also did Trafalgar Square and enjoyed a bit of London, but our minds were on our return home. The country boy had gotten a little taste of culture, thanks to his wife Pilar.

Pilar and me at the Acropolis in Greece,
showing off our new leather and suede clothing purchased in Turkey.
November, 1968.

TransCentury

January-February 1969

Since I did not immediately find a job of interest to me when we returned home, I decided to accept a short-time position offered by one of the first of what would later became known as " beltway bandits," agencies that sought government contracts to carry out specific assignments.

TransCentury was somewhat of an avant-garde group made up of a few well-known cerebral types who had set up their offices in a storefront in the most economically deprived area of Washington, D.C. No one had a private office, and everyone worked around long folding tables. The lights were naked bulbs hanging from the ceiling, but the work *atmosphere* was extremely stimulating. The work itself was not that great, however, but at least it kept me busy and earning a bit of money. I was part of a team of a half a dozen or more persons, quickly trained, and sent out to specific areas—chosen by lot in selected cities—to evaluate the work of the Office of Economic Opportunities (OEO).

We went from door-to-door in our prescribed area and attempted to interview whoever answered the door, using a predetermined set of questions. One could write a book about the types of people who were interviewed and their answers, but I'll leave that to someone else.

We did a test run in Washington, D.C., and then I was sent to Duluth and Minneapolis—in the dead of winter—as well as Nashville and Atlanta. Since I finished ahead of time, they also asked me to go to Charlottesville.

Thank goodness. I had good feelers out about a job in Latin America when I'd finished and did not have to continue with more of the same.

During this time, Pilar had headed south to Ecuador. She had originally come to the U.S. to spend a month or two traveling. She now returned, two and a half years later, married and having circled the globe while living and visiting in 14 countries. She missed her family, and they missed her. We would meet up again in Colombia, where I'd found a new assignment.

The only other thing of importance to report, here, is that this was the period when I began to have problems with flying as a result of several un-related incidents. On a flight from Malaysia to Thailand, we hit some clear-air turbulence that caused the plane to abruptly fall several thousand feet. Soon thereafter, two IVS friends of ours lived through a crash landing in the northern part of Thailand. While going from Israel to Turkey, we flew into a brutal storm over the Mediterranean Sea. And finally, several of my flights during the above-mentioned work took place in midwest snow storms. It was a difficulty I would have to endure for the next 10 years or so—until I found a way to conquer it.

International Development Foundation

Colombia and Ecuador

April 1969 - April 1971

The same friend, who had helped me find the job with IVS, identified International Development Foundation (IDF), a New York City-based non-profit agency that focused on programs in Latin America. They had obtained a grant from USAID and were putting together a team of five persons for a program in Colombia, which seemed just right for me. Agrarian reform was a hot topic in Latin America, and they were looking to train Ministry of Agriculture employees to form cooperatives to work the new lands being offered to them. The director was an American. His deputy was from Uruguay and the two trainers were from Peru. I had a job that was split between administration and field work.

Prior to going to Colombia, we spent a couple of weeks in Guatemala to get a firsthand look at some indigenous cooperatives in an area near Lake Atitlan. One of the interesting factors about these cooperatives was that they had been formed by the local foundation FUNDACEN (Fundacion del Centavo, or the Penny Foundation as it was referred to in English). While it was a Guatemalan institution, the idea for forming it had come from Sam Greene, a retired New York businessman living near the lake. He came up with the idea that the indigenous population needed access to capital in order to improve their economic situation. If someone were to provide them a loan, they would have to repay only pennies a day—if they worked as a group rather than individually. He provided the initial capital to test out his theory. It worked, and the rest is history. FUNDACEN was formed to institutionalize the process and it is still operating today.

I think it important to note that when we visited the cooperatives, it was 1969. FUNDACEN had been operational since 1963, twenty years prior to the first loans that Nobel Peace Prize winner Muhammad Yunus began giving out in Bangladesh. Moreover, almost at the same time, similar operations were being initiated in Mexico (FMDR, now FUNDAR) and in the Dominican Republic (FDD). By 1972, others had sprung up throughout Central and South America, and a consortium of these groups, SOLIDARIOS, was incorporated in the Dominican Republic in 1972. It was briefly headquartered in Guatemala (1975-77) before moving back to the Dominican Republic. Yunus certainly did a great deal to promote and expand micro-enterprise activity worldwide, but I would strongly contend that Sam Greene and the SOLIDARIOS agencies should have been identified as being the innovators of the idea and the initial practitioners. Yunus, whom I first met at a SOLIDARIOS-sponsored conference in Toronto in 1988, was, and is, a wonderful salesman, but he is not the "father" of micro-enterprise, as he is commonly called.

Following the orientation, it was on to Bogota, Colombia, where I was forced to find a house on my own. Thank goodness Pilar liked my choice when she arrived from her stay in Ecuador. Although the furniture was probably not to her liking, it was supplied by USAID, so I couldn't be faulted on that part.

The humorous part of her travel to Colombia happened at the airport in Quito—when she tried to leave. At that time, married women were not allowed to leave Ecuador unless they had written authorization from their husbands. Given it was her first experience as a married woman, she had totally forgotten about that regulation. Thankfully, the extended family had enough connections in the right places to get that overlooked since she was traveling to meet me, and an exception was made in her case. It caused some discomfort on her part, but I for one got a good chuckle out of it.

We moved quickly to put together a training program with the Ministry of Agriculture. After the initial selection of sites was made, the field work was divided among three of us, with the other two getting the brunt of the it, since I had some administrative responsibilities. It was very much a learning experience for me. Never having done this type of work before, I was basically "playing it by ear." I never did get to the point where I felt completely comfortable or confident about it.

This part of the work required me to spend a considerable amount of time in small villages, many of them without electricity or running water. It brought back memories of my Peace Corps training experience in Patzcuaro, Mexico, with the major difference that Colombia had a history of political violence. Many men openly carried arms, not only in the rural areas, but in the cities as well. The mixing of guns and alcohol was definitely a concern that surrounded us at all times.

After several months of this, I spoke with the Chief of Party about my concerns. As a result, my responsibilities in the field were curtailed considerably and my administrative activities were increased.

At the same time, problems began arising within the Ministry of Agriculture. It became increasingly obvious that our time in Colombia would be reduced. In the latter part of 1969, several of us flew to Cuenca, Ecuador, to discuss the possibilities of transferring our efforts to assist CREA, a regional rural development agency that had requested the type of services IDF was offering. Subsequently, the USAID contract was modified to allow us to shift gears in midstream. In the end, the Chief of Party went to Honduras, his deputy remained in Colombia to finish off that contract, and three of us were transferred to Ecuador to initiate the new contract under the leadership of a Cuban American who had previously worked for IDF on other assignments.

Our end date was December 31st, but in view of the fact that Pilar was in an advanced stage of pregnancy, we decided it would be better for her to leave in mid-November and be with her family.

When I arrived in Quito in early January 1970, I was met by a family friend, who had been asked to give me a lift to Ibarra. When we reached

San Pablo, a beautiful lake about 30 minutes from Ibarra, he pulled the car off to the side of the road, and there waiting to welcome me, in addition to Pilar, were both of my brother and sister-in-laws, several nieces, nephews, and importantly, my father-in-law, with whom I'd had only minimal contact with in the past—and never as a son-in-law.

When the moment came to greet him, I gave him an "abrazo" and said, "hola papa, como estas." This was very significant as both my brother-in-laws addressed him as Sr. Bonilla and always used the more polite "usted" form of the verb, not the familiar form of the verb I used. I did so because it was the way I treated everyone else. I found it difficult trying to decide when I should use one and when the other. In any case, my father-in-law loved it and we became great friends.

My in-laws had brought along a basket full of Pilsener beer, bread, and cheese, and we had a picnic on the side of the Pan American highway before continuing on to Ibarra.

Pilar and I soon made our home in an apartment in Quito, so that we could be close to family and to the clinic where the baby was to be born. As fate would have it, this was possible due to the fact that the whole IDF team would be going through a planning process prior to establishing ourselves in Cuenca, though there were some back and forths prior to that.

Pilar's time came, or so we thought, at about 4:00 a.m. in the morning, We made our way to the nearby clinic where she was prepped for the birth. At 6:00 a.m., a woman came to the clinic who was literally giving birth as she came through the front door and took the last available room. Her doctor, who was also Pilar's doctor—and a relative—was aware that we had also made reservations in the Hospital Voz Andes, run by the Evangelical Church. He asked if we didn't mind making the change. So off we went in a taxi with Pilar in her hospital gown, but it wasn't until 1:00 p.m. or so when Lorena del Pilar Finnell Bonilla came into the world. It was a real coincidence and a real blessing that by pure chance the birth could happen in Ecuador, among family and friends, instead of Colombia.

Some twenty or so years later, when Pilar and I were invited to a social event at the Ecuadorean Consulate in New York City, I struck up a conversation with an American woman sitting beside me. I soon learned that she was also married to an Ecuadorean and had a child born in Quito. When I asked, "How old," she indicated "21."

I said "Mine too, on February 24, 1970."

"What a coincidence," she added, "That's the same date as my son. Where was your daughter born?"

I answered, "Well, she was supposed to have been born at the Clinica Pichincha, but someone arrived at the last moment, and took her room. We had to go the Hospital Voz Andes instead."

The woman smiled broadly and countered, "I was that someone."

What an amazing coincidence to meet her after such a long time and in such a circumstance!

Maybe because it was Ecuador, or because I benefited from what I'd learned in Colombia. Or maybe it was because my assignment in Ecuador was to be mainly administrative, but my job situation was definitely more enjoyable than what it had been in Colombia. It was also challenging and a very positive learning experience. For instance, during our stay in Quito, we had the time and opportunity to work with a consultant, who helped us design a PERT (Planning, Evaluation & Review Technique) Chart for the work we were about to undertake. PERT charting was a technique NASA had developed in order to physically map out and see the various activities in an interrelated manner, as well as a better way to calculate and manage the timing. It was extremely interesting and proved to be invaluable in the implementation phase.

On another occasion later on, following an intense period of work and nerves were a bit frayed, we were led through a team-building session by a consultant who was skilled in this technique. It took an entire evening and into the wee hours of the morning to get things settled, but it was well worth the process. Another excellent learning experience.

Our relationship with CREA was a very amicable one. The training we provided for their field workers, who in turn were training the smaller farmers, and helping them work in a more cooperative manner, was extremely successful in a very short period of time. CREA was responsible for the rural development in the southern part of the country, both in the Andes region as well as the Amazon basin (Oriente). We had the opportunity to test the processes with a wide range of ethnic groups.

I particularly remember a trip all four of us took to the Oriente. We traveled south on the Pan American highway for a couple of hours before turning onto a gravel road for a short distance, when we could go no further. From there we went on foot, on a trail that was so saturated with water and mud from recent rains that we had to take care where to step for fear of sinking up to our knees in the sticky mess, which each of us did on more than one occasion. While we traversed only a relatively short distance, this part of the journey took us an agonizing four hours. We ended up in a small village in the middle of nowhere, one that had no hotels, restaurants, or amenities of any kind. Dinner was an old rooster that we paid a woman to cook for us, a meal that challenged our teeth and growled in our stomachs for the remainder of the night. We slept, if you can call it sleep, on a hard wooden floor covered by our ponchos.

At the break of day, we continued our odyssey on donkeys with wooden saddles, which we covered with our ponchos to make them slightly more comfortable. The trip down the mountain and into the jungle was the saving grace of the trip. It was one of the most incredibly beautiful visual experiences I've ever had. We were surrounded by lush vegetation dripping with raindrops from the night before. The flowers, multi-colored, gorgeous, and many times covered with indescribably nasty-looking insects, were often viewed at close range when the trail narrowed. The scenic valleys and rivers also provided a feast for the eyes.

Physically, however, the eight-hour trip was grueling, and I swear that nothing, absolutely nothing in my life, has ever felt so good as dismounting from my donkey. After another night of sleeping on a wooden floor on our ponchos and doing some visiting at the project site, we returned all the way back to Cuenca the next day.

All-in-all, the time in Cuenca was a very positive experience, but when my two-year contract came to an end, I again felt that I needed to move on in order to continue in pursuit of my career. Given that Washington, D.C. seemed to be the hub of international development activity, we headed directly there. The opportunity of learning a new planning technique, experiencing important team-building procedures and being part of a very successful rural development program, made the time well worth the investment.

Lorena celebrated her first birthday in Cuenca. While she did not yet have any "friends," we gathered some of our friends and a number of children we knew and made a "piñata." Not ever having done it before, I decorated a clay pot and filled it with candy, but it was so sturdy that even I couldn't break it. We ended up handing out the candy to the children.

Cuenca also represented a first for me—my first earthquake. It hit off shore in the early hours of the morning—a loud boom—much like the bombs we heard in Laos. Pilar immediately yelled, "Terremoto" and ran to get Lorena and take her out of the house. It took me several more minutes to react, and as I exited the bedroom, definitely not dressed for going outside the house, I noticed the very large clay pot that decorated the hallway was rocking very slowly from side to side. I was mesmerized by the movement and waited until it finally tipped over and crashed into pieces. By then the earthquake was over, except for several days of aftershocks.

International Voluntary Services (IVS)

The People Network Washington, D.C.

May 1971 - June 1972

Having been in contact in Laos with International Voluntary Services (IVS) volunteers Stan and Laurel Druben, Pilar and I set up camp on the living room floor of their apartment in the Southwest area of Washington, D.C.. We would stay there, about four or five blocks from the Capitol Building, until we located a two-bedroom apartment in the same complex.

My job search did not last long. One of my first contacts was with the headquarters of IVS in Dupont Circle. They offered me the post of Program Director, and I took only 24-hours to talk it over with Pilar and accept.

The large contracts that IVS previously had with USAID in Laos and Vietnam terminated with the conclusion of the U.S. participation in that war. And while there was still a money flow, it was not enough to maintain the number of volunteers that were previously serving. From a high of 300-plus volunteers, there were only 100 or so in Algeria, Indonesia, Laos, Libya, Morocco, Yemen, and Zaire. My work consisted of trying to develop new country programs, as well as expanding the funding sources. Neither of these were easy assignments—particularly the latter.

While identifying opportunities for volunteer activity was not difficult, it was both time consuming and expensive. IVS, in particular, did not have funding for the start-up costs. Fund raising also required an investment of a considerable amount of unrestricted monies, and competition for funds from churches, foundations, corporations, and individuals was fierce.

At the same time that I was being challenged with those duties, the Drubens, whom we saw on a daily basis, approached us one evening after dinner with an idea. Being the seat of the national government, there were a lot of comings and goings of people in Washington D.C. It was reported that the average person lived there for just a little over two years. This made it very difficult for an individual to meet others with similar interests, so the Drubens came up with the concept of offering a service, for a small fee, that could provide the connections, be it in the area of sports, chess, sewing, dancing, the arts, singing, or cooking—among other interests.

After many, many evenings of knocking the idea around, we decided to pool what little money we had and incorporate The People Network. Countless hours were invested in developing the processes and procedure, preparing written materials and generally getting ready to open the doors. We initially printed and folded 15,000 flyers and hand-delivered all, to avoid postage, by sneaking into any number of apartment buildings and going from floor to floor to slip them under people's doors. At the same time, we rented a one-room office on Connecticut Avenue, three block from the White House, and we were in business.

To make a long story, short, it was a wonderful idea, but unfortunately it was an idea well ahead of its time. We were attempting to put a sort of Face Book on the map some 35 years before the circumstances allowed, so we lost our opportunity to become billionaires. On the positive side, we received an amazing number and percentage of returns. *The Washingtonian*, a well-read local magazine, ran a story on The People Network, as did the magazine section of the *Los Angeles Times*. Cable stations were just beginning to appear, and one in Chicago, wanted to talk with us. Unfortunately, we didn't have enough funding to fly to Chicago. While the responses had been good, we needed considerably more volume to make The People Network not only profitable, but operational. Had the internet existed and had private computers been as common as they are today, things might have been different, but we could not attract other investors, so we had to shut the doors of The People Network.

Pretty much at the same time, IVS was no longer able to offer me employment due to money difficulties, so it was job-hunting time once again. Fortunately, the next opportunity, Private Agencies Collaborating Together, was waiting for me.

Sometimes we learn more from experiences that are unsuccessful than from ones that succeed. I'm sure many elements from the time spent with IVS Washington and The People Network fit into that category. In addition, IVS provided my first opportunity to work in the headquarter offices of an international development agency, and to interact with a Board of Directors. And I got a taste of the realities of fund raising. The People Network turned out to be a real hands-on seminar on the topic of "creating a new business."

Private Agencies Collaborating Together (PACT)

New York City

July 1972 - July 1979

During the last couple of months or so in Washington, D.C. I had been asked to represent IVS at a series of ongoing meetings that were taking place to create a new nonprofit that would promote collaboration and coordination among international nonprofit organizations. Private Agencies Collaborating Together (PACT) had been formed on paper, and a large grant was being negotiated from USAID to make it operational. Robert O'Brien was designated as its Executive Director and I became available soon after the grant was approved. I immediately interviewed for the only other position that was being filled at that time, Associate Director, and within days I was hired.

I had always said that nothing, not job opportunity, not money, absolutely nothing could entice me to live in New York City. Well, Pilar, Lorena, and I were off to New York, and as of this writing, we have been living in the suburb of Larchmont for 39 years and counting. The selection of Larchmont, which is a choice area northeast of the City, situated on the Long Island Sound, came about due to an offer from one of the Board Members of IVS. He was a retired Presbyterian minister and indicated that he was going to live in Bangladesh for a few months. He said we could live in his house if we agreed to pay a pro-rated amount of the taxes and utilities. That worked out to be $400 a month—not bad for a five-bedroom, three full-bathroom home located at the end of a cul-de-sac with a tree-lined trail bordering the back yard. Moreover, the "few months" turned out to be four years.

The commute to the City was an easy 35 minutes, culminating at Grand Central Station, just three blocks away from the PACT offices, which were across the street from the United Nations headquarters.

We soon found out that Larchmont and some of the surrounding communities were filled with U.N. ambassadors, consuls, other diplomats, businessmen and women from all over the world, and French families taking advantage of the French school in Larchmont. We began to socialize with a wide-ranging group of these individuals, as well as with families who'd lived in Larchmont for generations. While some of the international crowd were in the United States for only short tours of duty, others were more permanent and formed a core group of friends we continue to see frequently to this day.

Pilar especially thrived in this type of atmosphere, as did Lorena, who was growing up with others who were bi-and tri-lingual and who traveled often. Importantly, the security of my job allowed Pilar to dedicate herself to Lorena and the home during this period and not be distracted by the need to seek employment.

It was an exciting time for me as well. I was co-founding an important nonprofit organization and helping build it from scratch. Bob O'Brien, was not only my boss, but he also became a good friend. We worked easily together to create the framework of the consortium, both organizationally and philosophically.

The Board of Directors was made up of representatives of the 25-30 member agencies, plus others from outside the PVO (private and voluntary organizations) community, and very early on we began to add NGOs (nongovernmental organizations) from Latin America, Africa, and Asia to the membership.

Another important aspect for me personally was the opportunity to have a much closer working relationship with USAID. While my work experiences with IVS and IDF were both largely financed by USAID, I was not involved with the funding side of things, only the operations. In PACT's case, I actively participated in maintaining, reporting to, and upgrading the relationship with USAID in Washington, D.C.

Furthermore, my daily activities brought me into day-to-day contact with the U.S.-based PVO community, such as CARE, Save the Children, OXFAM America, Accion, Meals for Millions, and Africare, both in terms of one-on-one exchanges and a never-ending number of conferences on various topics.

However, the mainstay of my responsibilities related to the creation and maintenance of a process that would fairly distribute and disburse the approximately $4.0 million a year that USAID was providing for collaborative projects and programs in Latin America, Africa, and Asia. Since these funds were earmarked for the agencies that were affiliated with PACT, the most important part of what we did was to set up an independent Project Selection Committee of five persons who were knowledgeable about international development and the role of nonprofit agencies, but who were not associated with any of groups we would be funding.

While the concept was very solid, it proved to be the most difficult one to sell to the agencies that had bought into the creation of PACT. Over time, however, and many discussions, it was fully instituted and did avoid conflicts of interest and pressure being applied on staff to fund projects that did not meet the established guidelines regarding collaboration, impact indicators, administrative costs and the like.

Although I was still not comfortable with traveling, I had little choice but to accept multiple trips within the United States and many to Latin America. I also got my first introduction to Africa, visiting Kenya, Zambia, and Botswana, near the end of my tenure with PACT.

Importantly, in terms of where my profession took me later, I was able to establish very close ties with SOLIDARIOS and its 15 or so affiliated agencies, as well as with such solid organizations as SERVIVIENDA and FUNDAEC in Colombia, FEPP in Ecuador, and Esperanca in Brazil. Particularly significant to me was the opportunity to assist SOLIDARIOS in the establishment of their Development Fund, which began to give loans to their affiliates for micro-enterprise activity.

By 1979, PACT had eight permanent employees, and my position had been elevated to that of Deputy Executive Director. But, again felt the moment had come to move on—almost seven years to the date when I began.

I wanted to take advantage both of the many contacts I had made over time with the Latin American NGOs, and my knowledge of the resource side of the equation, to see if I could create some synergy. Since the PACT experience had provided me with a fairly high-profile position within the U.S. international development community, I felt I could use that as a springboard. What I soon found out was that maintaining that momentum without the advantage of controlling the purse strings to a significant "pot of money" would not be as easy as I thought.

The Resource

Larchmont, New York

July 1979 - May 1987

Having made my decision to leave PACT, I sent out notices offering my services to any and all comers, and while I had left with "nothing in-hand," I soon found myself on an airplane to Kenya, Liberia, and Senegal under a contract with USAID/Washington. I had decided to call my fledgling firm The Resource, and I was charged with the task of taking a look at the worthiness of local nonprofits to be subjects of USAID funding in general terms. Since I already had a good handle on Latin America, and some PACT experience with groups in Zambia, Botswana, and Ghana, this was an assignment to expand on that knowledge base. It was also an assignment that stretched over several years.

Other clients during that first half-year were USAID/Costa Rica—to provide fund-raising assistance to two local agencies—and two of PACT's U.S.-based affiliates—for general programming and fund raising assistance. All of these assignments, while part-time in nature, were more than just one-shot consultancies.

Consortiums had become a hot topic in the PVO community, so given my experience with helping to found PACT, 1980 brought with it a long-term commitment to assist COERADO, a grouping of evangelical agencies located in Canada and the United States—and other assignments with new consortiums in Costa Rica (ACORDE and FOV), Honduras (FOPRIDEH), and Guatemala (ASINDES). PACT was the contractor for the groups in Costa Rica and Guatemala. Other regular consultations included SOLIDARIOS, Save the Children, the Pan American Development Foundation, the Experiment in International Living, and the Consortium for Community Self-Help.

From the third year on, things really began to explode, including contracts with USAID offices in Guatemala, Honduras, Ecuador, Jamaica, and Peru; work for local nonprofits such as Servivienda (Colombia), FEPP (Ecuador) and FMDR (Mexico); church development agencies like Lutheran World Relief, Mission Aviation Fellowship, and United Methodist Committee on Relief; U.S.-based nonprofits such as Esperanca, Agricultural Cooperative Development International, and Meals for Millions; children's agencies, including Christian Children's Fund, Compassion International, Save the Children, and World Concern; a Canadian agency called HOPE International; and the Council on Foundations. One of most unique opportunities involved working with members of the Cherokee Nation in North Carolina.

I had any number of experiences during these times, both humorous and serious. On one occasion, when I was undertaking a three-day fundraising seminar for more than 50 local nonprofit agencies in Panama, I found myself seated on a platform in front of a large crowd during the kickoff of the event, which was being covered by both print and television media. Immediately following the preliminaries, three young ladies approached me and suggested I retire to the restroom and take off my pants, so they could repair them. It turns out that the entire seat of my pants had come unsown. We all got a big laugh out of that.

On a more serious note, when I was spending a month in Jamaica, I decided to take a Sunday morning stroll from my small hotel in Kingston to a larger one three blocks away to purchase a *Miami Herald* newspaper. It seemed like a simple enough task, but after advancing the first block, I knew I'd made a mistake, but it was too late to turn back. Gone were the hordes of people who were packing the streets during the work week, gone was the vehicular traffic as well. Replacing them were gangs of young thugs—selling drugs—I learned later—and saying menacing things to me all along my trek to the hotel. I did make it without incident, and, after purchasing my newspaper, I took a taxi for the three-block trip back to the hotel.

Another scary incident took place in Honduras as Kris Merschrod and I were conducting the final data-gathering interview at the rural headquarters of a large banana cooperative. We had made the appointment in advance and traveled down a long, single-lane road to their office, where we were met outside by a group of four or five campesinos. They led us inside to a room with a small conference table. As we sat down, the President of the cooperative took out one of the largest pistols I've ever seen, laid it on the table in front of himself and said, "Now what was it that you fellows wanted to talk about?" I forget what I answered, but I do remember that it was the shortest interview we had during the evaluation.

While on a trip to the Altiplano of Bolivia—12-14,000 feet above sea level—to evaluate the micro-lending programs of a local nonprofit agency, I had another experience that was somewhere between scary and ridiculous. Since I was viewed as an important visitor with ties to monetary resources, two Board Members of this institution decided to show me the projects rather than allowing staff members to do it. Unfortunately, neither one had a clue about where they were going, but off we went, at the crack of dawn. Traveling what seemed like forever, we drove across huge expanses of flat nothingness before seeing any kind of civilization. Stopping in a small village that would make my home town in Indiana look like a metropolis, my hosts asked for directions. This same scene was repeated several times over, after which I insisted that we return to La Paz. They finally had to acquiesce, as none of the places we visited had a place to eat, nor more importantly, a gas station, and the tank was hovering near empty. You can imagine the tenor of my report. The only positive aspect of that particular assignment was that I was spared from being forced to eat the local cuisine and therefore did not get sick, something that often happened during visits to places well off the beaten path.

When my consulting days were over, I had undertaken assignments with more than 75 organizations, and connected with another 350 indirectly, in 25 countries worldwide—over an eight-year period. Some of the assignments were short, some called for spending a month at a time in a given country, but most were ongoing relationships. In the majority of cases, I worked on my own, but from time to time I was assigned anywhere from one to three others to assist me in getting the work done.

The tasks were extremely varied and challenging. I provided management advice, helped with program planning, wrote proposals, evaluated programs, designed operational systems, helped put several national consortiums of NGOs on the map, undertook regular program oversight, did multi-day training events, interviewed candidates for new positions, and made recommendations for hiring. On two occasions, I was given the thankless task of firing the field representatives of U.S.-based agencies and taking charge of the local office for a short period.

The downside of this phase of my professional life was the travel. During the last years of the consulting activity, I had an average of 325 billable days per year, and I was away from home approximately 60-70% of the time. On more than one occasion, I would wake up in the morning and have to think for awhile before remembering where I was.

The upside was that it forced me to overcome my fear of flying. A good friend of mine, who had totally given up flying, began seeing a psychologist. He asked me if I wanted to start seeing the same person. I thought about it for awhile and came to the conclusion that this person was going to charge me $250 an hour to tell me that I had to come to grips with the reality that only an extremely low percentage of flights terminate in crashes. And the recommended solution would be that I would have to convince myself to sit back and relax. I decided to save the money and just do it. To this date, I can stay calm in even the roughest of turbulence.

One example of how I was tested during this period relates to a flight I took within Honduras to visit a project site in the northern part of the country near the border with Guatemala. There was no airport in that small village, so I was catching a ride with Mission Aviation Fellowship, a nonprofit agency with pilots who regularly fly into hard-to-access areas around the world, and service other nonprofit agencies. We were in a single-engine, seven-seat Cessna, and I was occupying the co-pilot's place. It felt weird taking off from a major airport in such a small plane. Once airborne we were never more than several thousand feet above ground, barely making it over the various mountain ridges encountered along the way. After a couple of hours of this, we reached our destination, but in order to land we had to make several low passes over the pasture—just missing the electricity lines each time we did so—to scare the cows away from the area where we eventually touched down. It was lots of fun.

The other advantage of frequent flying was that the accumulation of large amounts of mileage allowed me to fly first class or business class all of the time. I must admit, I got spoiled and very much enjoyed it.

In the end, however, the constant travel became a bit too much. It had come to the point that, when I walked into several major hotels in various capitals of Latin America, the doormen and registration desk employees would address me by my name before I even presented my credentials. I used a particular car service to and from the airport so frequently that they once surprised me with a stretch limo—at the regular price—just to give me a treat. The drivers taught me all the short cuts to and from the airports when there was traffic. On one occasion, I was met at the airport in Panama and ushered through the diplomatic entry point by someone who had no reason to know that I was arriving and had no reason to meet me. I never did figure that one out.

By then, I knew I needed a change. My final consultancy made that all too clear. I had received a call from the Asian-American Free Labor Institute (AAFLI) in Washington. D.C., wanting me to go to Sri Lanka and advise a large tea-growers association on aspects of becoming more financially self-sufficient. It would be a month-long trip, but I really didn't want to do it, in spite of the fact that a close friend of mine had highly recommended me.

To discourage them, I quoted a daily fee that was substantially higher than that which was accepted by the government contract they were operating under. They didn't even flinch. I then told them that, unlike other consultants, I charged for every day I was away from home, including flight time, Saturdays, and Sundays—whether I was working or not. They found that acceptable as well. I ended by stating that I required business class or first-class airline accommodation for a trip of that distance. Again there was no problem. In the end, I had to go.

It turned out to be a very interesting assignment, but I was totally exhausted when I got home. During the trip, I decided to start my own nonprofit organization.

As fate would have it, even before I could get the incorporation paperwork started, I received a call from CARE, who wanted me to go to Bolivia to fire their country director and put things in order. This time I did not negotiate, in spite of their insistence that I take on the assignment and their unhappiness that I would not relent.

I thought, again, that my experience base, my considerable knowledge of the players, my reputation as someone who could get things done, and my large network of contacts within the community of funding agencies would allow me to become operational and successful within a relatively short amount of time. Little did I know how wrong I was, and I soon found out who were, and who were not, my "real friends."

Relaxing at the home of a friend in Costa Rica
after a meeting of representatives of consortia in Honduras, Guatemala,
El Salvador, and Costa Rica.

Another trip to Costa Rica
when Pilar (second from left)
got to come along.

Discussing fund raising in Colombia
with a group of nonprofit leaders.

The staff I recruited to help with the training in Colombia.

The Students who attended
the fund-raising training session in Colombia.

Second Annual Meeting of Nonprofit Consortia
held in Cali, Colombia.
I am standing in the middle.

Ceremonies in Sri Lanka—my last Consulting job.

More ceremonies in Sri Lanka.

The Resource Foundation, Inc.

New York City

May 1987 - To Date

The shift from The Resource to The Resource Foundation, Inc. was a more gradual transition than a radical change of modus operandi. In fact, it took a considerable amount of time before most people fully understood the transformation. I was still operating out of the basement of my home. I was still contacting many of the same people, and I was still seeking to do many of the same things I'd done before. The biggest differences were that I was not traveling as much—and the flow of money had been severely curtailed.

Be that as it may, the second half of my 47-year career in international development had begun. I initiated this phase of my adventure with the encouragement, and the total support and involvement of my life partner, Pilar. I was convinced it was the right thing to do, and was resolved to see it through to the end. I was extremely naïve in terms of how difficult it would be and how severely my ability to persist would be tested.

I should explain, in more detail, why I decided to create The Resource Foundation. It goes far beyond just getting tired of traveling. It was focused on my interest in local nonprofit agencies in Latin America.

During my tenure with PACT, and even more so while I was consulting, I had begun to lobby very hard on behalf of local nonprofit agencies. I was convinced that they offered a more effective and permanent response to poverty within a given country. They had the language ability, they understood the local ambience and politics, and they knew their own people much better than anyone from the outside could—no matter how much training they had undertaken. Moreover, the beneficiaries felt more comfortable with individuals from their own country. What they lacked was access to financial resources in the United States.

Just think about it in reverse terms. How would you react, for example, if a group of young persons from, say France, Spain, or Germany, who spoke uneven English with a heavy accent, arrived in your small town or neighborhood and wanted to organize you to deal with economic and other problems affecting you. I'll bet your reaction would not be a very positive one—no matter how well meaning they were.

In the early to mid-1980s this message began to be pushed at all of the major conferences and meetings where international nonprofit agencies, governmental officials, and multinationals gathered. No matter what topic brought the group together, it was inevitable that the "southern" agencies—those from the developing nations—would say it was time for the "northern" agencies—those from the developed countries—to change their role. It was time for the southern agencies to become the driving force, the implementers, and the doers, and the northern agencies should take a back seat and become supporters and providers of resources.

Invariably, everyone would nod their heads in agreement, and the minutes of the meeting would indicate that all were dedicated to bringing that change about. The only problem was that the southern agencies were the only ones that followed through. To this day, the northern agencies in the United States, in large part, have refused to change the way they operate.

As I noted earlier, during my Peace Corps days this was one of the lessons I learned at that time, so I needed no further convincing that it was the right way to do things. That's why I had pushed for including local nonprofit agencies among the membership of PACT. It is why I lobbied, whenever possible, to include local agencies among the collaborative relationships that PACT was funding. It is why I focused as much as possible on local nonprofits during my consultative assignments. It is why I had such a close relationship with SOLIDARIOS and its 15-20 affiliates throughout Latin America, as well as with the consortia in 4-5 countries, and individual agencies everywhere. It is why I had a reputation for being the "go-to" guy for local nonprofits and why, for many, I was their champion and spokesperson in the United States.

One of my favorite stories about the oft-times misguided role of the expatriate advisors relates to a project that was undertaken on the coast of Ecuador in the early 1960s by an organization that shall go unnamed. The great minds that put this one together had decided, obviously with little or no consultations with the local populace, that what the poor fishermen in Esmeraldas needed was a modern facility to fast-freeze their fish so that they could be sold on a nationwide basis rather than just locally to those who could access them soon after they were caught. They convinced one of the local cooperatives about the merits of this idea and then spent tens of thousands of dollars to construct the plant before it occurred to anyone that 1) there were no refrigerated trucks in the country to transport the frozen fish; 2) even if there had been, there were no modern supermarkets with the freezers needed to store the fish once they arrived; and 3) even if there had been, not even the well-to-do families had freezers in their homes at that time. Poetically, even the freezer plant itself, which was built too close to the ocean, was eventually washed out to sea.

I chose to start The Resource Foundation in May 1987, after many conversations over an extended period of time with Padre Alberto Jimenez of SERVIVIENDA and Enrique Fernandez of SOLIDARIOS— among others. Most importantly, it was Pilar who not only gave me her full support and encouragement, but who also provided many key suggestions about how to develop the organization.

The Goal

The primary purpose of The Resource Foundation was, and is, to provide vital services to the local nonprofit agencies needed to gain access to international funding sources, as no one else was electing to offer. Even today, 24-years later, The Resource Foundation has only very limited competition in its particular operational niche.

The Beneficiary Agencies

As I began to recruit the initial affiliates of The Resource Foundation, there were two key elements I was looking for in the agencies— "self-help and sustainability." It was my belief, and that of many others, that real development will only take place if the beneficiaries themselves are totally involved in and are investing something into the process in the form of money, labor, and/or materials. Moreover, they need to participate intimately in the planning, administration, and execution of all aspects of the project. If it is a low-cost housing project, they must be consulted about the design, then help build the homes, as well as pay for them. If it is a micro-enterprise program, they must repay the loans from their earnings. They must be the "owners" of the project in order to have any hope that results will be sustainable and permanent.

In addition to looking for local nonprofit agencies committed to these two concepts, I was also seeking to assist groups that manifested strong executive leadership, had well-placed boards of directors, exhibited proven administrative capability, were financially stable, focused on innovative programs, benefited low-income persons, showed interest in gender, ethnic, and other types of equality, and had a high regard for the environment.

By the end of 1987, there were nine such organizations that had agreed to pay the annual dues in exchange for the services that The Resource Foundation would be providing. Of those groups, two—SERVIVIENDA and FUNDAEC—both of Colombia, are still active today.

The number of agencies affiliated with The Resource Foundation has now grown to 45. Their program focuses include Low-Cost Housing, Urban and Rural Micro-enterprise, Sustainable Agriculture, Environmental Protection, Basic Education, and Job Skills Training, Health Care, and Potable

Water and Sanitation.

These affiliated agencies, and the approximately 125 other associated agencies The Resource Foundation also assists with a lesser set of services each year, are located in 27 Latin American and Caribbean countries.

The Programs

The programs of The Resource Foundation's affiliates reflect the qualities listed and are extremely diverse in nature. In the beginning, I was able to draw upon the contacts I had made during my days with PACT and others that I worked with as a result of my many consultative assignments. The persons who managed these programs were pioneers in their respective fields of endeavor and founders of the organizations they were leading. They became icons, which many others sought to emulate—and still do. These were exciting and very stimulating times, and the participants were eager to work with, and benefit from, the type of services The Resource Foundation was offering participants.

For example, Padre Alberto Jimenez, who was so intimately involved in the creation of The Resource Foundation, founded SERVIVIENDA in Colombia in the late 1960s. I met him soon after. They are producing 15 prefabricated and very attractive houses each day. These units, which cost approximately $2,500 each, are affordable by even the lowest-income families thanks to a credit plan that has a 95% repayment rate. Built of cement slabs, metal, hardwood, and tile, the homes are simple, sturdy, attractive, easily transportable and can be erected in four hours by the families that purchase them.

The Fundacion Mexicana para el Desarrollo Rural (FMDR, now FUNDAR), was one of the pioneers in the area of micro-lending, along with FUNDACEN in Guatemala (also affiliated with The Resource Foundation). Led by Arturo Espinosa from the early 1960s through the 1980s and beyond, it offers a program composed of training, technical assistance, and credit. They provide instruction in the agricultural area, as well as for job skills such as carpentry, weaving, canning, and more, including small business management—cash flow, accounting, cost control, production, and marketing—and the use of credit. Many of their clients are women.

Juan Demeure created DESEC in Cochabamba, Bolivia, in 1972. Its focus is to work with dispersed, indigenous communities, combining environmental education, protection and technology with improved farming techniques, all of which lead to higher yields, increased self-reliance and greater quality of life. The programs address water conservation and management, soil erosion, terrace farming, use of solar energy for greenhouses, and family homes, crop rotation, animal husbandry, composting, and reforestation.

Accredited high-school degrees are provided by the FUNDACION ORIGEN in Chile for low-income, at-risk youth. It was founded in 1987 by Mary Anne Muller, a former Miss Chile, who is just as beautiful on the inside as she is on the outside, and she has created a model program that many have since copied. In addition to a regular degree, Origen also offers vocational training in trades such as carpentry, metalworking, farming, and animal husbandry. And it involves the students in environmental and community building activities. Ninety-five percent of the students find employment immediately following graduation, or are accepted into universities where they continue their education.

Mujeres en Desarrollo (MUDE), founded in 1979 in the Dominican Republic and directed for almost all that time by Rosa Rita Alvarez, is dedicated to improving the quality of life for rural and urban women and their families. To date, it has impacted the lives of 50,000 persons through microcredit programs, maternal, infant, reproductive health care, and more recently with HIV/AIDS education and prevention for adolescents. MUDE also addresses issues of self-esteem, leadership, and increased participation of women in community affairs.

On an annual basis, The Resource Foundation is currently channeling an average of approximately $50,000 to each of 150 agencies such as the ones described. These monies help finance more than 200 projects that, directly and indirectly, impact on five million disadvantaged individuals in

25 countries in Latin America and the Caribbean.

A few success stories, described by the individuals benefitting from the abovementioned programs, can be found in the attachments.

The First Six Months

I sought the assistance of a lawyer friend and neighbor to handle the legal part of incorporation, and he agreed to do it at half price. Actually, the work was done by one of his colleagues, who knew very little about nonprofits, so I ended up having to counsel him. Bottom line, it was done in a couple of months, and the IRS 501(c)3 classification came through not long after that.

On paper, the initial Board of Directors was made up of the lawyer friend, Pilar, and yours truly. However, I moved quickly to expand that list to others who I thought could help us during the original period. Of those, Larry Prince, a new friend at that time, and businessman, was the first one I recruited, and is the only one who is still a Director today. Alberto Jimenez is now an emeritus member of the Board. The 10 Directors met for the first time in November 1987 in our home, followed by a light, catered meal arranged by Larry's wife Judy.

The others included a contact of mine in Canada, another located in Europe, a businessman on the west coast, and two well-known persons living in the Larchmont area. Three other local residents were soon added . Today, the Board of Directors is made up of 23 extremely capable and well-placed individuals, many of whom who have served for more than 15-20 years and can take a large degree of credit for the success The Resource Foundation has attained.

In addition, an Advisory Committee of three persons was formed: Robert O'Brien, former Executive Director of PACT; Tom Fox, Director, NGO Office, Council on Foundations; and William Moody, Program Officer, Rockefeller Brothers Fund.

I also moved quickly to find an accounting/auditing firm. Maier,

Markey & Menashi (now Maier, Markey & Justic) took me "under their wing," and are still providing The Resource Foundation with much-needed, high-quality professional services at an affordable price.

During the first six months, my energies were focused on a few consultative activities to keep monies flowing and remain solvent, as well as some initial fund-raising that totaled $57,000 by the end of 1987. My daughter Lorena donated the first dollar. In addition, I began creating my own Directory of 660 international funding sources in the United States, Canada, Europe, and a Notebook of 20, three-to-five page "blurbs" about different aspects of fund-raising—in both English and Spanish.

I graduated from my trusty electric typewriter during this period by purchasing a small Radio Shack computer, one that was obviously much less sophisticated than ones available today, but it was helpful, though exasperating until I figured out a few things. After laboriously typing in the names, addresses, telephone numbers and bits of information about the hundreds of funding agencies for the Directory, the machine crashed, and I lost everything. In fact, it happened twice more before I found out from Radio Shack that no single file could extend beyond 20 pages. Once I knew that, I easily found a way to divide up the Directory into different sections, each with 20 pages or less, but not before it severely tested what little patience I have.

The Board of Directors

The selection and the involvement of the Board of Directors would prove to be extremely critical to the development and survival of The Resource Foundation, as I would basically be working on my own for ten years before the next full-time person joined the staff. I needed to be able to count on Directors who would be involved.

In the beginning, I reached out to persons I knew and I thought would be sympathetic to the objectives of The Resource Foundation, irrespective of whether they had any Latin American or international development experience. I was looking for those who would be willing to actively contribute both monetarily and otherwise. I had no interest in anyone who just wanted to lend me their "name" for our letterhead. I was, and still am, an avid proponent of the 3 G's—Give, Get others to give, or Get off the Board.

Larry Prince was the Chairman of the Board for the first six years, and after the initial period of getting organized, a system of staggered, three-year terms was established, a system that continues to this day. Officers (Chairman, Secretary, and Treasurer) were similarly elected for three-year terms. In this case, however, these individuals could not be reelected as officers until sitting out at least one term.

Another important measure was the annual appointment of an Executive Committee of nine persons to review and approve the actions of the Executive Director on a bi-monthly basis and report back to the full Board at the time of the Annual Meeting.

Several of the persons that were recruited during those early years decided not to continue for one reason or another, but over the years, The Resource Foundation began to attract others who had longer term commitments to the cause. Today, approximately 75% of the Directors have served at least 9-15 years, and one-third have been Board Members for 20 or more years.

Suffice to say at this point, The Resource Foundation would not have survived on my efforts alone—however dedicated I was to the task. The active and interested involvement and support of the various Directors over time has been a critically important factor in the process.

The Next Several Years

There were many important accomplishments during the next six to eight years, but these were basically very lean times and extremely difficult to weather. I could have easily quit at any time, and no one would have blamed me or thought worse of me. At one point, during a particularly down time, I remember looking skyward in my little basement office and pleading to God in a loud voice to please use me. There was no immediate response, but it made me feel better, knowing God was not going to forget about me. Besides, persistence had very much become my byword. I had no intention of giving up on a good idea.

Early in 1988, a wonderful Larchmont couple, Tom and Silvia Muldoon, held a wine and cheese get together in their home and invited all of their wealthy friends, including the then Mayor of the Village, who has been a faithful and important contributor to this day. It resulted in 30 new individual donors and a much needed $2,500. A year later, Joe and Lucy Maloney did something similar, attracting 100 new donors and another $7,500. The following year, we held our first of 19 major fund-raising events in the Larchmont Yacht Club, which we promoted as *Dancing on the Water*.

Dancing on the Water—a name coined by Judy Prince—turned out to be a real favorite for many supporters of The Resource Foundation. Thanks to Pilar's prayers, never once did it rain on this mid-June event. There were many extremely successful evenings, but not everyone was a fan of such an evening, and one of my favorite memories is that of a very good friend of mine at one of the early occasions. He was wonderfully captured in a classic photo, bored to death and studying his fingernails. Be that as it may, he never missed attending.

During this time period, the Board of Directors was expanded to 15 members, and the number of affiliates grew to 20. By drawing on former contacts, eight fund-raising seminars were offered to a large number of nonprofits in a similar number of countries. While the amounts were not large, new donors included Citibank, Texaco, Bristol-Myers Squibb, the Weyerhaeuser Foundation, and the International Foundation— among others. The average annual income was approximately $250,000.

The Realities of Fund-Raising. Some Lessons Learned

During the early stage of the Resource Foundation, I got a real taste of the realities of raising funds from institutional sources—principally foundations, corporations, and religious organizations—via proposal writing. I have selected just a few of those that had happy, but hard-earned conclusions. While reading these, however, one should keep in mind that intermingled with every success presented below, were anywhere from five to ten, and possibly even fifteen cases where the response was ruthlessly quick, extremely impersonal, and without a doubt, negative. As will be obvious, even the positive responses required a great amount of work, skill, and luck. The cases are genuine. "to protect the innocent." They are presented in first person, by he who "survived" them:

Case One - Assisted Success

—In May 1988, I sent a general request to one of the major banks.

—In December 1988, I got one of the oft-quoted, standard replies: "wishing us well with our fund-raising efforts."

—In June of 1989, 1990, 1991, 1992 and 1993, I tried again, each time with the same results.

—I'm ashamed to admit, in 1994 and 1995, I gave up and did nothing.

—In 1996, I had a shot of brilliance one day and remembered that my next-door neighbor, and faithful contributor, had a responsible position with this same bank.

—I sent in a new proposal and asked her to make a recommendation on our behalf. She was kind enough to contact not only the headquarters office in New York, but each of the general managers in four countries.

—In December 1996, we received a first year grant of $25,000, with the promise of more to come.

Case Two - Get Your Foot in the Door

—A review of the 1990 *Taft Directory* revealed a small foundation among the new entries, $500,000 of annual giving and some $10 million in assets.

—A March 1990 submission for BEST in Belize got a fairly quick turndown.

—An October 1990 submission for ARBOFILIA in Costa Rica, again got a quick turndown, but a follow-up telephone conversation found a Program Administrator with some general interest in our approach. Due to an unlisted number, this conversation was only made possible by a lot of detective work.

—A similar submission was made in May 1991, and follow-up telephone conversations indicated that while it was not going to fly, I should send some additional general information to them and that she would try to set up a meeting with the President and Executive Director of the Foundation at a later date.

—That meeting finally took place, a year and a half later, September 1992, after numerous telephone conversations every 60 days or so. The meeting was quite positive and, as a result, we were invited to submit a proposal for RODELILLO (now ORIGEN) in Chile. We did so immediately.

—Very likely, due to problems with availability of funds, our September 1992 submission was deferred from their January 1993 meeting, but it finally received a two-year, $20,000 grant at their May 1993 meeting—a little over three years after our initial contact.

—Normally, this might be the end of the story, but since the Executive Director of RODELILLO visited the U.S. in the Fall of 1993, I set up a meeting with the President and Executive Director of the Foundation, just to have them get to know one another. Also attending, by chance, was the sister of the President, who, together with him, also controlled a second small foundation interested in "the arts." The chemistry was just right. Things went so well that a Resource Foundation Board Member, as well, got invited to a Saturday outing with these same individuals, where many very personal stories were shared. As a result, we were invited to submit a proposal to the second foundation.

—In February 1994, this second foundation made a $6,500 grant for the art and music program of RODELILLO, and annual contributions have continued.

Case Three - Personal Communication Counts

—In July 1992, I found a very small, mid-western family foundation ($2 million in assets, and $120,000 of giving) listed among the donors of another non-profit agency. A check with the *Taft Directory* seemed to indicate that they focused their resources on Latin America.

—I sent them a small request for a fishing development program of DAI in Dominica, and got no response. Being a family foundation, they had no employees and answered no requests. After several telephone conversations, I found out in December that no funding would be forthcoming.

—In January 1993, I sent them a FEPP project for land purchase and agricultural development.

—Hearing nothing again, I began calling in April 1993, and did so monthly, as in each case I was told the foundation would be meeting in the near future.

—In September 1993, I called to say I would be available to meet them personally, letting them know I had a formal invitation from my alma mater (located near them). They declined the offer.

— In December 1993, the President of the foundation indicated that his wife had just had surgery (he explained the particulars), and that something would likely happen during the first quarter of 1994.

—I sent a get-well card and other materials, and began to call again in April 1994.

—In June 1994, the President indicated that his wife had misplaced our file and he asked if we would resubmit. We did so immediately.

—On August 3, 1994, the President finally called us to say they liked what we were doing, and that we would be receiving a $10,000 contribution.

—However, after a 45-day wait and still no check, I called to inquire and talked to the wife who had yet a new illness.

—On November 4, 1994, the check finally arrived, without any accompanying communication or fanfare from the wife.

—Annual communications and checks have continued to date.

Case Four - An Easy One

—In July 1994, I found a potential new source from among a list of foundations supporting another agency (assets of $21 million and annual giving of a bit more than $1 million).

—Among other interests they seemed to like family planning, and Brazil in particular, so I tried FESPERAN.

—In early November 1994, we received notice of a $24,500 grant.

—What is this? You go to the directory, identify an appropriate potential funder, write a proposal, submit it, and within a reasonable amount of time get a positive reply and a check? Is that how it's supposed to be?

Case Five - A Blind Date -or - A Fishing Expedition

—Just when I thought I had sent proposals to almost all the foundations interested in international programs, a new directory listed some X number of new ones.

—Taking advantage of having an intern during the Winter months of 1995/96, I mailed out general letters and information to at least 100 of these "marginal" prospects. The request was very general, accompanied with an "offer" to present a specific proposal.

—Several good things happened as a result of that mailing, but the one that comes most quickly to mind is a $7,500 check that arrived one fine day, three months later, without additional fanfare or proposals, asking us to apply it to three agencies that THEY had selected.

—More checks have followed.

If you have gotten this far and still have a good "gut" feeling about fund-raising, I would invite you to go back to the introduction of this section and read it again.

During the early period, I used to keep Larry Prince up to date on contributions. I can still remember that day I excitedly called him to report our first $25,000 donation from a foundation. Nowadays we regularly get checks or wires in the $300-$500,000 range, but I don't tell anyone about it until it comes time to write a weekly missive or a monthly update. Oh, how times have changed!

The Model and the Growth

Two critically important milestones took place in 1994, which would forever change the fortunes of The Resource Foundation. A short time before, Larry Prince and I had convinced a friend and former schoolmate of his, Bill Hockman, to join the Board of Directors. By 1996, Bill had become the Chairman of the Board. but he had been instrumental in making very important changes even before then.

Out of the blue, Larry invited Bill and me to lunch one day. I thought it was just a social affair. Little did I know the impact it would generate. The conversation turned to finances, which were always tight, and Bill started making notes on his napkin. Obviously, it wasn't a fancy restaurant. He then raised the concept of quotas for the Directors, meaning that every Board Member would be responsible for some amount of unrestricted funding per year. They could contribute some or all of this from their own pockets, and/or they could generate it from donations made by friends, foundations, corporations, or churches. We all did some more jotting and all agreed that $6,500 was an amount that would make a difference and that it was an amount most everyone could manage one way or another. The bottom line was that this meant that The Resource Foundation would have a basic amount of funds it could count on each year in order to maintain the organization.

That had a critically important impact on the well-being of the organization. However, the second action taken by Bill would prove to have an even more dramatic effect on the operations of The Resource Foundation.

Bill's company, Hockman-Lewis Ltd., did a considerable amount of business in Central and South America, providing all the elements one would need to operate a service station: gasoline pumps, air pumps, hoses, tools, and replacement parts. One of his major clients at that time was Texaco, which had a large chain of service stations throughout the region.

Bill invited me to accompany him on one of his periodical field trips to visit his local offices. We were able to cover four countries (Guatemala, El Salvador, Honduras, and Nicaragua) in a week's time. Each time, we also called on the local representative of Texaco, and Bill allowed me to make presentations about The Resource Foundation. In all cases, we found very fertile ground for the product we were selling.

The Texaco representatives were extremely interested in making contributions to local nonprofit agencies, as they could potentially get more "bang for their buck"—public relations and exposure—compared to supporting the programs of an expatriate agency operating in that country. The problem was that they knew very little about who the right groups to support were, and they had neither the time nor the expertise to find out. Their other problem was that the monies for philanthropy flowed out of headquarters, and there was a reluctance to go through all of the paperwork required by the U.S. government to do so. It was much easier to make donations to a 501(c)3 organization. We countered by offering to match them with quality agencies that could implement programs in the areas where they had interest, and to speak with Texaco in Purchase, New York, about the paperwork.

During our previous conversations with Texaco headquarters, we knew, in theory, they too would prefer to make contributions to local nonprofits. When we later explained that we could handle all the administrative procedures for a fair price, as well as monitor the programs and report back to them regularly in English, we had created a de facto tripartite model that could be implemented elsewhere. Corporate headquarters, corporate local offices and The Resource Foundation all had the potential for being winners, and the local nonprofits would be the beneficiaries.

It all seemed so simple, and it was. Moreover, it worked. Within a reasonably short time following that trip, Texaco monies began to flow through The Resource Foundation to all four countries we had visited.

Suddenly, we had a real product to sell to corporate America, a different one from what others were selling. It also came at a time when corporations were taking increased interest in Latin America, as evidenced by the fact that the size of their grants had begun to rise from the $1-$5,000 range to the $10-$25,000 range.

Following smaller successes with Abbott Laboratories, Chase, and Pfizer, the next major conquest came with Philip Morris International (PMI), and by 1997, The Resource Foundation's income had risen to $800,000. In the years that followed, the success rate would begin to quicken as a direct result of the model that had been developed during the one-week trip to Central America.

The relationships with both Texaco and PMI were also characterized by the amount of dialogue between them and The Resource Foundation. It went well beyond just a request for funding and the mailing of a check. There were regular telephone conversations and consultations. It was almost as if I were part of their staff. For example, when the Vice President for Corporate Social Responsibility retired several years later, the President of PMI organized a private party at a very upscale club for 80-100 employees (no spouses) in order to honor her. I was the only non-staff person invited. Even more significant was the fact that I was one of three persons invited to formally address the gathering and say a few words about her. The other two were the President himself and another high-ranking officer.

Another extremely important event took place during this period, which was unrelated to Bill Hockman's tenure as Chair. In August 1997, I was invited to the Dominican Republic by Enrique Fernandez, General Secretary of SOLIDARIO, to discuss a working relationship between them and The Resource Foundation. Enrique, who had been with SOLIDARIOS since the very beginning (1972), was about to step down, and he felt that the time was right to merge the two organizations. Although an agreement was reached to do just that, difficulties would occur in the future that did not allow the merger to come to fruition. Nevertheless, a strong partnership was produced that ballooned The Resource Foundation's membership to more than 40 agencies.

The Conclusion of Phase One - 1997

The first 10 years of The Resource Foundation had ended, a period during which I had been working alone, other than a couple of years of part-time assistance from Brooks Smith and volunteer inputs from college students during two summers. As I indicated, it was a time during which the Board of Directors played such an undeniable critically important role in terms of the Foundation's survival.

However, while The Resource Foundation came through this evolution in a solvent manner, I cannot say the same for the Finnell family. I was unable to take a regular salary during the first six or seven years. Even when I did begin to receive something on a monthly basis, it was not sufficient to cover our family's needs. Pilar was therefore forced to find meaningful employment to help keep our heads somewhat above water. She eventually turned to real estate, which she has been doing very successfully now for more than 20 years. Nevertheless, the Finnell family accumulated $300,000 of personal debt during this period, a condition that had not been erased by the passage of time. Hopefully, this reality gives testimony to just how much both Pilar and I believed in the concept of The Resource Foundation and how much we were willing to invest.

The Consolidation and Further Growth 1998-2010

In January 1998, I invited a young woman to leave a job at one of the major banks and help me take The Resource Foundation to the next level. An economist with NGO experience, she joined the staff two years later, in January 2000, followed by a lawyer in September of that same year. Both had Ecuadorean roots. Other staff members were added from 2006-2010, and any number of graduate and undergraduate interns have been recruited regularly from Princeton, Columbia, and New York University for short-term assignments.

Each time a new person was added, the Board of Directors supported my decision to expand, but not without voicing their deep concern about whether we could afford the additional expense. In each case, we were stretched to the limit but, in the end, we always found a way to complete the year with a small positive margin.

It should be obvious that The Resource Foundation is much more than any one person. It is a group of talented and dedicated individuals willing to work together, within the parameters of a vision established in 1987, to achieve a stated set of institutional goals. In addition to the critically important role assumed by the Board of Directors, the Staff that was hired, beginning in 1998, had also been instrumental to further growth.

While filling the various staff positions over time, my philosophy was, and still is, to find the right person and create a job that fits that individual's talents and experience. I specifically eschewed the way others normally operate, which is to create a position and look for the person to fill it. I looked for persons who were energetic and committed, persons that had good ideas, some relevant experience, and persons with language and other talents to add to the pool of tools we needed to be successful. It was easy enough to give this individual an appropriate title at the appropriate time, but much more important to ascertain whether that person could add something significant for the good of the organization. I'm pleased to say, in the great majority of cases, this manner of doing things has been extremely successful to the institutional growth of The Resource Foundation and its ability to provide benefits to those in need of our assistance. I'm particularly indebted to the following current staff members: Marcela Lopez-Macedonio, Maria Eugenia Vasquez, Aimee Soskowski, Anabay Sullivan, and Larissa Curado; as well as former employees Julia Love, Meredith Ahlberg, and Carmen Ilizarbe. Without their dedicated and caring inputs, we would not be where we are at this time.

The Resource Foundation not only survived during this development period, it survived extremely well. The entire staff thrived in a working atmosphere where each individual was allowed to contribute to the maximum, and were also involved in a plethora of activities.

Several very important events took place during the consolidation and growth period that began in 1998, and impacted on progress in different ways. The most important of these was an in-house, five-year Strategic Planning activity that we undertook in 1999. It was assisted by two Board Members, Ken Ricci and Carl Muñana, and it was the first such document The Resource Foundation had ever done. However, the plan itself was not as monumental as the realizations reached by the group as part of the process: Our donors were our clients, not just sources of funds. This seemingly simple acknowledgement changed the way we talked about the relationships and how we presented and promoted ourselves.

In the first instance, we began to refer to the manner of relating as a "partnership," where there was give and take, as opposed to a sterile environment—where one side or the other was "calling the shots." More importantly, it opened the door for the donors to tell us what their priorities were in terms of objectives, guidelines, countries, and agencies. They were not just waiting for The Resource Foundation to send them project proposals to consider. Very quickly it resulted in their suggesting local agencies to support—who were not among our members.

The passage of the Patriot Act during the Presidency of George W. Bush—with many new requirements for assisting local NGOs—further solidified corporations' need for The Resource Foundation's services. Today, support for non-affiliated agencies out-numbers affiliated agencies on a two-to-one basis, and many of the agencies we have recruited to be members in recent years have been selected from among those suggested by the donors.

All of a sudden, The Resource Foundation began to acknowledge that it was serving two distinct types of clients. On the one hand, we were continuing to assist a select group of nonprofit agencies in Latin America and the Caribbean, while at the same time providing a sophisticated and much needed set of services to our donor clients. These included the identification of local nonprofit agencies, the time-consuming due-diligence required by the U.S. Government in order to support local agencies, the preparation of project and program descriptions in English, the transmission of funds to the project implementers, the monitoring of the approved activities, the reporting back in English to the donor clients, and participating in their in-house staff-planning meetings.

If requested, The Resource Foundation also began to offer the possibility of undertaking formal evaluations, assisting with the preparation of public relations materials in Spanish, and arranging for volunteer inputs by local employees of the donor client.

In 2003, we began to sublet space from Ricci-Greene Associates (a Board Member), enabling us to be in one place for the first time. And in 2004, a second strategic plan was undertaken with the pro bono assistance of the prestigious firm of McKinsey & Co., thanks to a request made by Board Member Pedro Lichtinger of Pfizer Inc. It was an extremely well-thought-out, professional, and useful instrument, but it did not have the same impact on our methodology as the one we did in-house.

Another notable event that took place in this period was a three-day management-training activity in Costa Rica I negotiated with Texaco just prior to their merger with Chevron. With the $100,000 grant they provided, I was able to sub-contract with INCAE, the well-known Latin American management-training institution. They put together one of the most professional training events I've ever witnessed. It was attended by 30 executive directors and board members of nonprofit agencies from 15 Latin American countries. After paying for all the training and travel costs, The Resource Foundation was left with $25,000 of much-needed, unrestricted funding, and it led to our involvement in other training activities on a regular basis.

The Texaco Management Institute (TMI), as the event was named, was also memorable due to the fact that I was scheduled to fly to Costa Rica on the day after 9/11 in 2001, which I obviously did not do. But I did travel just three days later on one of the first international flights permitted to leave the country. I have vivid memories of the taxi ride to Newark Airport and seeing the still burning site of the towers from the other side of the

Hudson River, as well as making my way through the thousands of stranded travelers in the airport. They were sleeping on cots that had been set up in any available floor space. As the plane took off, another view of the smoldering pit was etched in my mind forever.

With a couple of exceptions, this period was marked by steady growth (15-30% per year), thanks to the further modification of The Resource Foundation's model and the advantage of the additional manpower. In addition, Carla Volpe Porter, and fellow Board Member Jose M. de Lasa, took the occasion in 2007 to rewrite our outdated bylaws.

In 2008, we were able to lease 2,000 sq. ft. of office space on our own at 35th Street, between 7th and 8th Avenues in New York City. While the Foundation continued to have a strong base of financial support from individuals in Larchmont, it was obvious that we had definitely become a NYC organization.

The only things that slowed us down were Philip Morris International's decision to do things in house after they moved to Lausanne, Switzerland, in 2008, (a loss of a $1.4 million account at the time), and the downturn in the world economy in 2009. Luckily, the result in each case was no worse than two years of flat budgets. There was no retreat, no retrenching, and no loss of staff.

In 2009, thanks to the keen interest and investment of considerable time on the part of Board Member Ruedi Laager, a new logo, tag-line, stationery, and newsletter format dramatically enhanced The Resource Foundation's image, while the web site went through a major upgrade as well. These changes received many kudos from one and all.

The Board of Directors was increased to 23 members and the annual quota per Director was raised to $10,000, as a result of a recommendation by then Chair, Carla Volpe Porter. As a result, my title was changed to that of President & CEO, and I was added to the Board of Directors.

Income grew from $1,000,000 in 1998 to $7,300,000 in 2010. Important new donors included Levi Strauss, Alcatel-Lucent, Citibank, Kraft Foods, Johnson & Johnson, ADM Software, American Express, the Tinker

Foundation, Kellogg, Deutsche Bank, Starbucks, Caterpillar, Dow Chemical, and ExxonMobil, among others, bringing to five, the number of major corporations utilizing The Resource Foundation as their sole channel of support for funding projects in Latin America. The number of small-to mid-sized foundations had also been on the rise, as well as large contributions from individual donors.

Importantly, Charity Navigator, an independent entity that ranks nonprofit agencies of all kinds in terms of their economic stability and spending habits, has given The Resource Foundation its highest rating—4-Stars—for the last four years, something only 8% of nonprofits have attained.

Further assisting the stability of the organization has been the establishment of an Evergreen Fund. A modest amount of almost $300,000 was raised and set aside for the purpose of helping The Resource Foundation get through periods of cash-flow difficulties during the year. Instead of either foregoing payment of bills, or seeking a bank loan—something that has never been done—we have been able to utilize small amounts of this Fund for a short period—as long as it was repaid before the end of the year. A sub-committee of three Directors was set up to monitor and approve the investment and use of these monies.

In a related move, Marcela Lopez-Macedonio's title was upgraded to that of Executive Director in 2010 and it was formally acknowledged that she was fully responsible for the day-to-day operations of the Foundation, allowing me to dedicate my efforts in working with the Board of Directors, identifying new sources of financial support, and promoting the Foundation through such activities as the Forum that we co-hosted with the United Nations Office for Partnerships (UNOP) in 2010.

My introduction to the UNOP was a rather unique one and almost didn't happen. One of our major donors highly recommended that I contact them, so after more than a month of attempting to set up a meeting with Amir Dossal, the head of that office, I arrived punctually on the hour of the agreed time, as is my custom. I was escorted to Mr. Dossal's office and was told that "he would be with me shortly." Upon receiving that same message for the fourth time over a 50-minute period, I informed the bearer of that information that I was leaving, and that Mr. Dossal could give me a call if he was serious about meeting. I stalked out of the room, adding that my title was Dr.—not Mr. Finnell. After exiting the building, I proceeded up 44th Street toward a place where I was going to have some lunch. Less than a block away, I felt a tap on my shoulder and turned to find the Chief of Office Operations. He asked if I would please return to meet with Mr. Dossal. I responded in the negative and continued on my way. After a few more paces, there was another tap on my shoulder. I turned to find the smiling face of a person who I was sure had to be Amir Dossal. He was so apologetic and so diplomatic that I could not stay angry, so we began our conversations as we continued along the way to where I was having lunch, with the Chief of Office following us and taking notes. We walked slowly and took an indirect route, thereby finishing our business without going back to his office. We have been good friends ever since, and I would love to have a movie of the three of us setting the stage for the very successful forum in that unique manner.

The Current Situation

In the past, when I conducted training activities regarding nonprofit organizations, the very first point that I normally made was the fact that there is only one difference between a for-profit corporation and a nonprofit corporation, and that relates to how profits are handled. Both types of corporations must operate in a manner to make a profit, but while the for-profit entity shares part of its profits with its investors, the nonprofit organization uses its year-end excesses to further strengthen its base. The bottom line is, however, that the successful nonprofit must have profits.

I'm pleased to say that while The Resource Foundation is not rich, it is solvent today, and it has been careful to have more income than expenditures each and every year.

It is rich in terms of both Board Members and Staff, and while The

Resource Foundation must eschew publicity for the most part (highlighting the donors and the beneficiaries), it has been able to gain a very excellent reputation among its partners. Both the funders—corporate, foundations, and individuals—and the nonprofit agencies it assists very actively seek us out and highly value our services.

That having been said, the Staff can be characterized as anything but complacent, as all are constantly seeking ways to improve the status quo and stay on the cutting edge. No one is resting on the laurels already won. We got to the point, where we are, by taking a unique idea and running with it. However, a few others are beginning to follow and unless we move ahead forcefully, we will get swept back into the mainstream of things. We definitely do not want to take that path; we are doing everything we can to maintain our front-runner position.

Not The End

This sort of brings things up to date, but if you were looking for neat and tidy ending, I do not have one to offer. My goal was to write my memoirs, and during that process relate how a country boy from a small town in Indiana managed to go around the world a couple of times, meet and mingle with presidents and other heads of state, have ambassadors as personal friends, and end up living in one of the largest cities in the world, while continuing to feel like that kid from North Manchester, Indiana.

I only hope God will give me enough additional years to be part of the further building at The Resource Foundation and to write a sequel to the above. Until then, I leave you with this anonymous quote:

> Press on! Nothing in the world can take the place of persistence. Talent will not: Nothing is more common than unsuccessful persons with talent. Genius will not: Unrewarded genius is almost a proverb. Education will not: The world is full of educated derelicts. Persistence and determination alone are omnipotent.

May 31, 1987

To My Daddy,

Embarking on a
new phase
of his career,
for believing in
the good of the human
heart.
I Love You
Your proud daughter,
Lorena

Honoring the Texaco Foundation for their $200,000 contribution in 1997—the year we established the Corporate Model. Maria-Mike Mayer, Manager of Corporate Contributions, and Rachel Speltz, Senior Public Relations Coordinator at the time of our Annual Fund Raising Event.

Dancing with my daughter Lorena at that same event.

A group of Ecuadorean friends attending the event for Texaco.
Pilar is third from the left (standing).

IV

Some Additional Musings

With Attachments

While I did not seek the following accolades, I also find it difficult not to be proud of something Tom Fox wrote about me in 2006 in support of the Sargent Shriver Humanitarian Award. It is particularly relevant given, my life work. He wrote:

> I believe that [Loren] can take considerable credit for the U.S. development community's acceptance of the fact that development will remain very slow in many poor countries if their own civil society is not empowered and supported, through the vehicle of NGO....Finnell's Resource Foundation has both encouraged and helped many individual and corporate donors support non-U.S. NGOs in ways they previously felt was too complicated or risky. He has really 'written the book' on this practice, a huge accomplishment."

Those words from Tom, a highly respected and well-known person in the field of international development, and The Sargent Shriver Humanitarian Award, presented to me in the historic Senate Caucus Room by former Senator Harris Wofford from Pennsylvania—co-founder of the Peace Corps and advisor to President Kennedy and Martin Luther King, meant the world to me, as did the words of keynote speaker Senator Christopher Dodd of Connecticut.

I thank The Friends of Ecuador, a Washington, D.C.-based alumni group of former volunteers and friends, for having nominated and lobbied my candidacy for the award.

Given my family's long association with Manchester College, I am also beholden to them for the Philanthropy Award given to me in 1997, as well as the Alumni Award in 2002, and most importantly—the Doctor of Humane Letters that was bestowed in 2008. I am only sorry that my parents did not live long enough to enjoy that wonderful moment.

I cannot conclude these memoirs, however, without reiterating how much I cherish the family ties that I have benefited from over the years, which have helped shaped my life. While I was largely independent my entire adult life, my parents were there for me every step of the way, including visiting me in Ecuador during my Peace Corps days and in 1967, coming to Laos, following my marriage to Pilar. Family also means my sister Anne, who also visited us in Ecuador and who was there for Pilar and me when our lives were turned upside down right after our marriage. She and her family have been part and parcel of so many good memories over the years at enumerable family get-togethers in Wisconsin, Indiana, Michigan, Massachusetts, and Virginia. And the epitome of family is the Bonilla Madera clan in Ecuador, too numerous to count, but incredibly loving and supportive to a person.

Finally, family includes the many good friends we have made in Larchmont and the surrounding area, and who have so faithfully supported us when we needed it most: Nicola and Margarita Arena, Alain and Marie Francoise Concher, Fabian and Leny Cordova, Gerard and Irene de Barros Conti, Jose and Maite de Lasa, Jose and Josefina Diaz, Frank and Alina Diaz-Balart, Phyllis DiMenna, Sheldon and Phyllis Evans, Carolyn Gallaher, Norman and Adriana Glickman, Reudi and Alix Laager, Gustavo and Rosa Marcela Lopez, Clemente and Emperatriz Machuca, Joe and Lucy Maloney, Jean and Gisele Masse, Tom and Silvia Muldoon, Cristian and

Maria Angelica Ossa, Gustavo and Fina Perez-Ramirez, Tim and Carla Porter, Larry and Judy Prince, Ken and Annalea Ricci, Federico and Carmen Gloria Riesco, Marlon Salazar and Yolanda Vivanco, and Rene and Maria Angelica Toro, to name but just a few.

But most of all, family means my wife Pilar, my daughter Lorena, and my niece Maria Eugenia—who lived with us for many years. Without their constant support and love, I would not have been able to accomplish what I have done.

Pilar and me celebrating
on a warm summer evening.

Barbecuing with a few of my buddies on Father's Day:
Federico Riesco, Chilean, and former high ranking official at the United
Nations; Alain Concher, French, Senior Vice President of L'Oreal and
long-time treasurer of The Resource Foundation; Gerard DeBarros Conti,
French, former officer with Bayer; and Larry Prince, fellow gringo,
Chairman of J.B. Prince Company, and First Chairman
of The Resource Foundation.

Loren Finnell

Manchester College

Office of the President
604 E. College Avenue
P.O. Box 365
North Manchester, Indiana 46962-0365
Tel. 260-982-5050   Fax 260-982-5042
www.manchester.edu

July 11, 2007

Loren Finnell
The Resource Foundation
158 West 27th Street, 10th Floor
New York, NY 10001

Dear Loren:

On behalf of Manchester College, with enthusiastic support from the Faculty and the Board of Trustees, I invite you to receive an honorary doctorate from Manchester College, a doctor of humane letters, *honoris causa*. We invite you to receive that degree at our commencement on Sunday, May 18, 2008 or at a date that better suits your busy schedule if necessary.

You have honored Manchester College with your life and career, each of which reflects fully the goal that we articulate in our mission statement: "to graduate persons of ability and conviction." Your early work in international development right after college and your leadership with the Resource Foundation have provided enormous support for persons in Latin America and elsewhere. You have secured and shared significant funding with agencies that address complex issues of reproductive health education, child labor, food production, infant health, housing, micro-enterprises, libraries, hurricane relief, and orphans.

More than most, you understand the essential role of "seed money" to turn dreams into practical realities. You have intensified the respect for the Resource Foundation by providing recipients of your grants with education about accountability and management as well as funds for direct services.

If you can join us for the 2008 commencement on Sunday, May 18, we would ask that you offer a very brief charge (7-9 minutes) to our 200+ graduates that day. Your message would be fully of your own choosing, and I know that all of us who are present will benefit from hearing it as well as the graduates.

I hope that you can accept our invitation. I have heard so much about you, but have not yet had an opportunity to meet. Along with many others here, I cheered your selection as the 2006 Sargent Shriver Award by the National Peace Corps Association. While Manchester cannot offer the marble and grandeur of Capitol Hill, we will welcome you back warmly to the campus with its old oak trees, red brick buildings, and trusty fountain!

If you have any questions, please feel free to contact me.

Sincerely,

Jo Young Switzer
President

154

—Photo by David Cook

Accepting a doctorate of humane letters, honorius causa, from Manchester College, Manchester, Indiana, May 18, 2008.

—Photo by David Cook

Lorena, President Jo Switzer of Manchester College, me, and Pilar.

—Photo by David Cook

Left to right: niece Valerie Frantz, my sister Anne, daughter Lorena, Pilar, me, and nephew Andy celebrating my Honorary Degree.

Left to right: Senator Chris Dodd of Connecticut; John Riggan, Member of the National Peach Corps Association's Advisory Council; me—Loren Finnell, Executive Director of the Resource Foundation; and Harris Wofford, co-founder of the Peace Corps with Sargent Shriver, and former Senator from Pennsylvania.

COMMITTEE ON APPROPRIATIONS

SUBCOMMITTEES:
LABOR, HEALTH AND HUMAN SERVICES,
AND EDUCATION

FOREIGN OPERATIONS,
EXPORT FINANCING AND
RELATED PROGRAMS

WASHINGTON OFFICE:

2329 RAYBURN HOUSE OFFICE BUILDING
WASHINGTON, DC 20515
(202) 225-6506
FAX: (202) 225-0546

DISTRICT OFFICES

WESTCHESTER
222 MAMARONECK AVENUE
SUITE 310
WHITE PLAINS, NY 10605
(914) 428-1707
FAX: (914) 328-1505

ROCKLAND
15 THIRD STREET
NEW CITY, NY 10956
(845) 638-3895
FAX: (845) 638-3497

Nita M. Lowey
Congress of the United States
18th District, New York

September 14, 2006

Loren Finnell
The Resource Foundation
158 West 27th Street, 10th Floor
New York, NY 10001

Dear Loren:

I would like to congratulate you on being the recipient of the National Peace Corps Association's 2006 Sargent Shriver Award for Distinguished Humanitarian Service. The leadership and dedication to service you have demonstrated through your accomplishments makes you a truly worthy recipient of this award.

The time you have committed to providing assistance to developing areas of the world is invaluable. From serving in the Peace Corps in Ecuador to founding the Resource Foundation, the efforts and successes you have pioneered have helped to bring about much advancement to Latin American and Caribbean countries. The Resource Foundation has been such a successful and noteworthy organization, and through your leadership has become essential in helping to provide for education, housing, job skills and more throughout a variety of nations.

I commend you on your tremendous accomplishments. Again, please accept my warmest congratulations and my best wishes for the future.

Sincerely,

Nita M. Lowey
Member of Congress

NML:ds

Loren Finnell

Kenneth and Jane Cole
1732 Valdez Dr. NE
Albuquerque, NM 87112
28 March 2006

National Peace Corps Association
Washington, D.C.

Ref: Shriver Award

Dear Friends,

We are delighted to support the nomination of Loren Finnell, founder and Chairman of
The Resource Foundation for this year's Shriver Award. We have known Loren since
1964, when we were all volunteers with Peace Corps in Ecuador, and over the years we
have had many opportunities to observe his remarkable achievements with The Resource
Foundation.

Very specifically, through the foundation he has:

- Delivered many millions of dollars to community-based organizations in much of
  Latin America.
- Obtained resources for these purposes from small charities and philanthropies that
  otherwise would not have supported efforts outside the U.S.
- Built a cadre of supporters among friends, neighbors and business executives,
  which has enabled the foundation to expand its efforts year after year.

This effort is in the very best tradition of the Peace Corps, as the immediate result is that
he is helping others to help themselves, in communities very much like those in which we
worked as volunteers.

Brief comments about us are in order so that you can appreciate that this testimony is
well-founded. Ken Cole worked many years at the Inter-American Development Bank,
and was responsible for a grants program that supported NGOs in Latin America whose
focus was to enhance the income level of families in poverty. In this work he came to
know many of the organizations that then and now received vital support from The
Resource Foundation. Jane Cole after Peace Corps obtained a Masters Degree in
Anthropology, worked with Hispanic immigrant communities, and in ongoing contacts
with Loren and his family has seen directly his continued commitment to the work he
began many years ago in Ecuador.

We have over the years known many persons who were volunteers in the Peace Corps, and can think of no one who has done more than Loren Finnell to help the communities to which Peace Corps is dedicated. He is exceptionally deserving of the Shriver Award.

Please feel free to contact us if you feel additional information is in order.

Yours truly,

Ken Cole

Jane Cole

CC: Loren Finnell

Loren Finnell

INTERVINE INCORPORATED
1700 SECOND STREET
SUITE 200
NAPA, CALIFORNIA 94559

March 31, 2006

National Peace Corps Association
1900 L Street NW
Suite 205
Washington, DC 20036-5002

Dear Sir/Madam:

It is my honor and pleasure to provide a few words in support of the nomination of Mr. Loren Finnell of The Resource Foundation for the Shriver Award for Humanitarian Service.

I have known Loren for more than fifteen years. Our initial introduction came via a Foundation in Chile with which I had become involved. Fundacion Origen had founded an Agro-ecological school for high school age children coming from extremely disadvantaged socio-economic backgrounds. Origen was an agency of The Resource Foundation and they suggested that I get in contact with Loren in the United States so that I might make my donations to them through a tax-deductible US organization.

After one conversation with Loren, I was completely enamored with the foundation he had created to provide a "hand up, not a hand out" to a variety of agencies doing critically important and diverse work throughout Latin America. When Loren asked me to join the Board of Directors of The Resource Foundation, I immediately accepted. I am pleased to say that today The Resource Foundation represents more than 100 nonprofit agencies in 23 Latin American and Caribbean countries. These agencies find financial support for self-help, socio-economic activities in the areas of primary health care, micro-enterprises, sustainable agriculture, environmental concerns, low-cost housing and education. More than 5 million individuals are helped by the work of The Resource Foundation.

Fundacion Origen is a perfect example of the success of Loren's vision. Over the past several years, Loren has secured grants from corporations and foundations in North America to fund the educational and micro-enterprises work of the school. With this seed money, the school is now well on its way to self-sustainability through the production and sale of honey, breads, jams and other products produced at the school. The recent construction of a small restaurant and hotel on the property created an additional revenue source. On my last visit

TELEPHONE: 707.253.1665
FACSIMILE: 707.253.1152

inter vine

there early this month, I found a project that has almost achieved full self-sustainability. Origen is an educational facility that now graduates 100% of its students with high school diplomas and agricultural certificates, 60% of whom go on to college or further technical training. The other 40% enter directly into the work force. Besides the technical certification, all students are trained in problem solving and conflict resolution which directly impacts their families and communities. The school and its unique curriculum now serve as a template for other schools throughout the country and region. Loren and The Resource Foundation were absolutely critical to the success of Origen.

I often think about what it is that motivates someone to dedicate his life to those less fortunate than himself. While most of us stumble along working at our jobs, paying our mortgages, and raising our children, there are some rare and special souls who do all that *and* decide to dedicate their life to others, and oftentimes to others whom they will never meet and who will never even know their name. I have seen how the Peace Corps initially attracts, and then ignites these individuals, sending them out into the world as ambassadors of the Corps' good work.

Loren Finnell's lifetime of work embodies all of the great values of the Peace Corps. Loren has used his kindness, compassion, humor, and entrepreneurial spirit to improve the lives of millions of disadvantaged individuals throughout the world. With all that he has done, Loren has retained his modesty and optimism and the world is undoubtedly a better place because of his work. Today, after more than 40 years of dedicated service, tears still fill Loren's eyes when he witnesses a success at an agency.

It is with great pleasure and full confidence that I support the nomination of Loren Finnell for the Shriver Award for Humanitarian Service. Loren is the perfect embodiment of your award's objectives and I cannot imagine a more deserving honoree.

I thank you for your kind consideration.

Sincerely,

Colleen J. May
CEO

Loren Finnell

Thomas H. Fox
3435 34th Pl. NW
Washington, DC 20016
Tel. (202) 686-6581
FoxThomasH@aol.com

Date: April 27, 2006

Shriver Award
National Peace Corps Association
1900 L Street, NW, Suite 205
Washington, D.C. 20036

I am most pleased to second the nomination of Loren Finnell for the prestigious Shriver Award. I have known him well and followed his career closely since 1972, starting with his great contribution in helping to create Private Agencies Collaborating Together (PACT).

As the founder of The Resource Foundation, in itself an important contribution to Americans' support for community-based development, Loren Finnell is responsible for two very important accomplishments. The first is his role in making American development donors and practitioners focus on the particular needs and essential roles of non-governmental organizations (NGOs). Believing that there was too much emphasis on US-based NGOs, Finnell did some serious research on the topic and then created The Resource Foundation to exemplify that importance. I believe that he can take considerable credit for the US development community's acceptance of the fact that development will remain very slow in many poor countries if their own civil society is not empowered and supported, through the vehicle of NGOs.

Second, and related, Finnell's Resource Foundation has both encouraged and helped many individual and corporate donors support non-US NGOs in ways they previously felt was too complicated or too risky. He has really "written the book" on this practice, a huge accomplishment.

There is no doubt in my mind that Loren Finnell would be the ideal winner of the Shriver Award.

Sincerely,

Thomas H. Fox
Peace Corps, 1965-72 (Country Director, Burkina Faso; Deputy Regional Director)
USAID, 1978-82 and 1997-2001 (Director, NGO Office; then Assistant Administrator)
Council on Foundations, 1982-87 (VP, International Programs)

Still A Country Boy

FOREIGN POLICY ASSOCIATION

National Headquarters
470 Park Avenue South
New York, NY 10016-6819
Tel. (212) 481-8100   Fax (212) 9275/9276

October 27, 2009

Mr. Loren Finnell
President & CEO
The Resource Foundation
237 West 35th Street
Suite 1203
New York, NY 10001

Dear Ms. Finnell:

It gives me great pleasure to inform you that the Fellows Committee of the Foreign Policy Association has voted to invite you to become a Fellow. As the nation's oldest international affairs organization, FPA has a wealth of experience in programming events our Fellows find stimulating and informative. Enclosed is a fuller description of the benefits to joining the Fellows program.

We hope that you will accept our invitation to become a Fellow and join us for a reception in honor of Steve Forbes, President & CEO, Forbes, on Tuesday, November 24, 2009 per the enclosed invitation.

Sincerely,

Noel V. Lateef

Enclosures,

www.fpa.org

165

ATTACHMENTS #4

Rockefeller
Brothers Fund
Philanthropy for an Interdependent World

April 30, 2006

Shriver Award
National Peace Corps Association
1900 L Street, Suite 205
Washington, DC   20036

Dear Shriver Award Panel:

I am writing in support of the nomination of Loren Finnell for the 2006 Shriver Award.

I have known and worked with Loren for more than thirty years. During this time, I have been a program officer at the Rockefeller Brothers Fund, and I have had many opportunities to become acquainted with Loren's important efforts.

I was in charge of the Fund's grantmaking in Latin America and the Caribbean in the 1970s when Loren helped establish and develop Private Agencies Collaborating Together (PACT). I remember our involvement with and grants to PACT. I also recall the special qualities that Loren brought to the challenge of establishing an international consortium of private development agencies that sought to cooperate in their efforts to respond to economic and social needs in Africa, Asia, Latin America and the Caribbean. Not only did he have experience in communities in rural and urban areas in Latin America and not only did he know Spanish as a native would speak, but also Loren's ways of relating to people at the grass roots and people in the assistance organizations nurtured PACT and its innovative programs. Loren was modest and humble; he built trust; he thought of how local people could take full advantage of experiences and lessons learned.

In more recent years, I have followed the Resource Foundation, established in the late 1980s, by Loren. At that time, I certainly thought a need and a niche existed for such an undertaking to help strengthen grass roots nonprofit organizations in developing countries; however, I was not sure whether it would be possible to raise sufficient funds to reach a minimum critical mass for a long term involvement. Well, Loren proved it could be done.

RBF | 437 Madison Avenue New York, New York 10022-7001 PHONE +1.212.812.4200 FAX +1.212.812.4299 WEBSITE www.rbf.org

The mission of the Resource Foundation continues to be highly valuable, working as it does to support more than 100 nonprofit agencies in 23 Latin American and Caribbean countries. Loren put together an engaged board and hired committed staff. Then, he and his team worked very hard and, over time, designed innovative fund raising strategies that have led to considerable amounts of support from new sources for indigenous efforts. The role and impact of the Resource Foundation have exceeded my expectations.

I admire the vision, leadership, management talents and dedication that Loren brings to the foundation. Moreover, as I have had opportunities to compare various approaches in development assistance, I attach particular importance to the mutually reinforcing strategies of the Resource Foundation through its grants, training, counseling and other services that, taken together, offer distinctly promising opportunities for indigenous organizations to gain self confidence and strength while actively carrying out their missions. While the grants and other services of the foundation are responsive to capacity building needs of the local agencies, the work of the Resource Foundation provides recognition and volunteer opportunities for donors, their staffs and others.

I wish to add a word about Loren when we were neighbors for four years. He and his family were at the top of my list of thoughtful and concerned people in the community. Loren showed a special quality of caring about neighbors and responding to needs—usually before others. His natural abilities encouraged cooperative action—time after time. His great sense of humor was a bonus!

I welcome this chance to express my full support and enthusiasm for the nomination of Loren Finnell for the 2006 Shriver Award.

Sincerely,

William S. Moody
Program Officer

wmoody@rbf.org

167

Making a presentation to the corporate leaders at, a Forum co-hosted
with the United Nations Office of Partnerships.

TRAVEL, mostly business related

Canada:
- Winnipeg: 50 – one time
- Toronto: 71, 88 – two times
- Ottawa: 74, 81 – two times
- Vancouver: 81, 81 – two times

United States:
- Little Rock, AK: 72 – one time
- Nogales, AZ: 64 – one time
- Phoenix, AZ: 80, 81, 84, 85, 86, 86, 88, 90, 92, 94, 95, 96, 97, 98 – fourteen times
- Carmel, CA: 77 – one time
- Santa Monica, CA – 77 one time
- Los Angeles, CA: 81 – one time
- Redlands, CA: 81 – one time
- Colorado Springs, CO: 80, 81,81 – three times
- Ft. Myers, FL: 84 – one time
- Miami, FL: 80, 87, 96, 97, 01, 03 – six times
- Atlanta, GE: 69 – one time
- Chicago, IL: 80, 02, 06 – three times
- Wheaton, IL: 66, 68, 81 – three times
- Indianapolis, IN: 97, 98, 00, 02, 08 – five times
- Boston, MA: 66, 75, 77, 79 – four times
- Duluth, MN: 69 – one time
- Minneapolis, MN: 69 – one time
- Bozeman, MT: 64, 89 – two times
- Charlotte, NC: 69 – one time
- Cheerokee, NC: 80 – one time
- Lake Junaluska, NC: 89 – one time
- New York, NY: 60, 64, 69, 71, 72 (resident for thirty-eight years) – five times
- Schenectady, NY: 72 – one time
- Akron, PA: 78 – one time
- Philadelphia, PA: 88, 11 – two times
- Nashville, TN: 69 – one time
- Brownsville, TX: 80 – one time
- San Antonio, TX: 84 – one time
- Houston, TX: 07 – one time
- Richmond, VA: 85, 85, 85 – three times
- Vienna, VA: 81 – one time
- Seattle, WA: 81, 81 – two times
- Washington, DC: 60, 66, 69, 70 (resident for one year), 72, 73, 74, 75, 76, 77, 78, 79, 79, 79, 80, 80, 81, 81, 82, 82, 82, 82, 83, 84, 84, 85, 85, 86, 86, 87, 88, 89, 90, 90, 91, 92, 95, 96, 97, 02, 04, 06, 08, 09 – forty-four times

Latin America and the Caribbean

- Argentina: 66 – one time
- Barbados: 90 – one time
- Belize: 85 – one time
- Bolivia: 78, 82, 83, 84, 84, 85, 86, 89 – eight times
- Brazil: 74, 78, 83, 83, 84, 84, 98 – seven times
- Chile: 66, 82 – two times
- Colombia: 65, 69 (resident for one year), 73, 74, 75, 76, 78, 79, 80, 81, 82, 83, 84, 84, 84, 84, 88, 90 – eighteen times
- Costa Rica: 75, 77, 79, 79, 80, 81, 85, 85, 86, 86, 86, 86, 86, 86, 86, 87, 87, 87, 87, 87, 88, 89, 90, 01 – twenty-four times
- Dominican Republic: 77, 80, 82, 84, 84, 84, 85, 85, 87, 90, 93, 97, 02, 07, 09 – fifteen times
- Ecuador: 64 (resident for two years), 69, 70 (resident for one year), 73, 74, 75, 76, 78, 80, 80, 82 (one month stay), 82, 83, 83, 84, 84, 86, 86, 89, 92, 94, 08 – twenty-two times
- El Salvador: 77, 97, 99 – three times
- Guatemala: 69, 69, 76, 77, 81 (one month stay), 86, 86, 86, 86, 86, 86, 86, 86, 86, 87, 87, 87, 87, 88, 88, 89, 89, 90, 93, 97 – twenty-five times
- Haiti: 81, 90, 91 – three times
- Honduras: 73, 77, 79, 81 (one month stay), 82, 82, 83, 85, 86, 86, 88, 97 – twelve times
- Jamaica: 83 (one month stay) – one time
- Mexico: 64 (one month stay), 78, 80, 85, 88, 91, 97 – seven times
- Nicaragua: 77, 97 – two times
- Panama: 75, 76, 80, 84, 84, 86, 90, 92 – eight times
- Peru: 66, 66, 78, 79, 82, 84, 89, 91 – eight times
- St. Lucia: 90 – one time
- Venezuela: 84, 98, 01, 07 – four times

Asia

- Cambodia: 68 – one time
- Hong Kong: 66 – one time
- India: 68 – one time
- Japan; 66 – one time
- Laos: 66 (resident for two years) – one time
- Malaysia: 67 – one time
- Philippines: 68 (one month stay) – one time
- Sri Lanka: 87 (one month stay) – one time
- Thailand: 66, 67, 67, 67, 67, 68, 68, 68, 68, 68, 68, 68, 68, 68 – fourteen times

Africa

- Botswana: 78 – one time
- Kenya: 78, 81 – two times

- Liberia: 79 – one time
- Senegal: 79 – one time
- Zambia: 78 – one time

Middle East
- Turkey: 68 – one time
- Israel: 68 – one time

Europe
- England: 68 – one time
- France: 68, 87 – two times
- Greece: 68 – one time
- Holland: 78, 81, 87 – three times
- Italy: 68 – one time
- Spain: 68 – one time

Loren Finnell

WILLIAM JEFFERSON CLINTON

January 4, 2011

Mr. Loren Finnell
Founder, President & CEO
The Resource Foundation
Suite 1203
237 West 35th Street
New York, New York 10001

Dear Loren:

I am pleased to invite you to become a member of the Clinton Global Initiative (CGI) — a community of international leaders committed to identifying groundbreaking solutions that reduce poverty, improve the environment, and increase access to health care and education around the world.

Throughout the year, CGI helps companies, nonprofits, and governmental organizations build partnerships that match cutting edge ideas with the resources needed to create real change. Our community is driven by a common belief that by working together, we can do more. I'm proud that CGI members have launched nearly 2,000 projects, improving the lives of 300 million people in more than 170 countries.

Membership culminates in our Annual Meeting, an invitation-only event for top leaders from around the world, which will be held in New York September 19 – 22, 2011. Since 2005, CGI's Annual Meetings have convened nearly 150 current and former heads of state, along with 15 Nobel Peace Prize winners and hundreds of top CEOs. Nearly 1,000 journalists cover CGI's Annual Meetings, as we recognize the progress that our members have achieved.

In the coming weeks, my team will be sending more information about CGI membership and our upcoming events. Please contact your CGI representative, whose card is attached, with any questions you may have.

I hope you are able to join us in this truly global effort.

Sincerely,

Bill Clinton

The Resource Foundation
Empowering Donors to Strengthen Communities

FACT SHEET

Mission

To empower individuals in Latin America and the Caribbean to have the skills, knowledge and opportunities to improve their lives.

Leadership

Loren Finnell, L.H.D., honoris causa, Founder, President & CEO
Marcela Lopez-Macedonio, Esq., Executive Director

Established

1987

Regional Focus

27 countries in Latin America and the Caribbean

Donor Services

Philanthropic advisory services include assistance in the identification of projects, presentation of proposals based on donors' interests and objectives, and the legal and operational framework for funds transfers, among others. TRF's work spans ten development areas: affordable housing, capacity building, cultural programs, disaster relief, education and job-skills training, environmental protection, health care and HIV/AIDS prevention and care, microenterprise, potable water, and sustainable agriculture.

Due Diligence, Reporting and Evaluation

The Resource Foundation's annual due diligence process includes a comprehensive evaluation of the proposed organization and project to ensure success and effectiveness. Its semi-annual reporting and impact measurement processes provide donors with detailed narrative and financial information on all projects supported.

Recognition and Accomplishments

- Awarded Charity Navigator's highest rating of four-stars for organizational efficiency and sound fiscal management in 2008, 2009 and 2010.
- Selected by Fidelity Charitable Gift Fund as one of four intermediaries that can facilitate international giving for its clients.

Impact

Thanks to donors' generous contributions since 1987, The Resource Foundation has provided more than $41 million to support more than 900 projects in 27 countries in Latin America and the Caribbean, which benefited more 31 million individuals.

Learn more about
The Resource Foundation
Visit our website ...
www.resourcefnd.org

Loren Finnell

The Resource Foundation
Empowering Donors to Strengthen Communities

About Us

The Resource Foundation is a leading U.S. nonprofit organization that facilitates philanthropic giving exclusively to Latin America and the Caribbean. Since 1987, it has been partnering with donors and effective, local nonprofit organizations in 27 countries to increase opportunities and improve living standards for the region's disadvantaged.

The Resource Foundation leverages its expertise, knowledge of the region, and multilingual capabilities to help donors optimize the impact of their philanthropy. It has pioneered effective giving to the region by supporting reputable organizations that work in all major development areas. Because many development issues are interconnected, its integral approach of supporting programs in education, health, microfinance, and other areas, ensures that lasting change is achieved.

The Resource Foundation has been credited with "taking a leading role in making U.S. donors and practitioners focus on the needs of non-profit organizations," as well as "writing the book" on encouraging and helping individuals and corporations to support their work.

Charity Navigator has awarded The Resource Foundation its highest rating of four-stars for its organizational efficiency and sound fiscal management for three consecutive years (2008, 2009 and 2010). This is an honor that only 14% of rated charities receive.

The Resource Foundation is also a founding member of the *Alliance for International Giving* together with Give2Asia and The King Baudouin Foundation United States. The Alliance was created to provide donors with access to a combined philanthropic network that spans the globe.

The Approach

Local Partners: The Resource Foundation (TRF) partners with nonprofit organizations (NGOs) that have direct knowledge of socioeconomic, cultural, and political realities in their respective countries and have built trust among targeted communities. TRF's affiliate NGOs utilize their knowledge and experience to ensure the sustainability and success of all projects.

Geographic Scope: The Resource Foundation's network includes 198 NGOs in 27 countries Latin America and the Caribbean. Based on its expertise, it has the ability to support development projects throughout the region.

Addressing Local Issues: TRF's affiliates work across ten major development areas: affordable housing, capacity building, cultural programs, disaster relief, education and job-skills training, environmental conservation, health care and HIV/AIDS prevention and care, microenterprise training and loans, potable water, and sustainable agriculture.

Funding Partners: TRF's supporters include individuals, foundations and corporations. Foundation and corporate partners include Alcatel-Lucent Foundation, American Express Foundation, Bank of America, Caterpillar, Citi, Deutsche Bank Americas Foundation, Dow Chemical Company Foundation, Johnson & Johnson, JP Morgan Chase, Kellogg Company, L'Oréal USA, Pfizer Inc., Quintiles, Silicon Valley Community Foundation, Starbucks, and The Rohatyn Group, among others.

Learn more about
The Resource Foundation

Visit our website ...

www.resourcefnd.org

174

The Resource Foundation
Empowering Donors to Strengthen Communities

PHILANTHROPIC SERVICES TO FULFILL CHARITABLE GOALS

Giving to Latin America and the Caribbean is not always simple – donors must deal with compliance, tax and efficiency issues, as well as complex matters that are unique to each country. Donors need an expert that understands their philanthropic goals and can help them navigate through the process to achieve a lasting impact.

The Resource Foundation (TRF) is an expert at facilitating charitable giving from U.S. donors to Latin America and the Caribbean. For over 23 years, donors have relied on TRF's knowledge of the region's nonprofit organizations (NGOs) and their programs, and its tailored philanthropic services to safely and securely support effective NGOs in 27 countries. Through its experienced, multilingual staff, TRF provides donors with individualized services. Among these are the following:

- **Strategic Philanthropic Advising:** TRF works with you to identify programs, strategies and projects that meet your philanthropic objectives. Whether you want to support programs that target a specific population, issue or country, we can help you define a strategy that ensures your contribution has the greatest reach.

- **Grant Management Support:** TRF also helps donors perform many traditional "in house" functions. TRF manages, tracks, and can coordinate additional support related to donors' grantmaking through regular grant tracking updates, liaising with donors' local employees for the selection and management of funded projects, periodic communication with grantee to monitor progress, and preparation of articles and informational documents related to funded projects.

- **Comprehensive Due Diligence Processes:** TRF researches and verifies that the proposed foreign organization and project meet all U.S. laws and practices for international grantmaking. Due diligence is conducted for all proposed projects and all funded organizations on an annual basis. TRF also contacts in-country representatives for additional information.

- **Grantee Identification:** Through its network of 198 organizations from 27 countries, TRF helps donors identify effective organizations that meet their charitable goals. TRF can also identify organizations outside its network, and/or facilitate funding to an organization previously identified by the donor.

- **Diverse Programmatic Portfolio:** TRF's broad portfolio reaches underserved populations throughout the region. Local NGOs implement innovative programs in 10 development areas.

- **Monitoring and Evaluation:** All grantees are required to submit semi-annual narrative and financial progress reports to TRF. Reports are analyzed, translated and sent to donors. TRF may also make site visits where it deems appropriate, or at a donor's request.

- **Visibility:** TRF collaborates with donors and local staff to ensure that support is communicated to appropriate media outlets and highlighted in corporate communications materials.

- **Transparency and Accountability:** TRF maintains tight cost-controls. Over 90% of revenues are applied directly to programs and services. Charity Navigator has awarded TRF its highest rating of four-stars for efficiency and sound fiscal management in 2008, 2009 and 2010. TRF is independently audited on an annual basis and all financial statements are available for review.

- **Tax-Efficient Funds Transfer:** As a 501(c)(3) public charity, donations made to TRF are fully tax-deductible as allowed by law.

Learn more about
The Resource Foundation

Visit our website …

www.resourcefnd.org

Loren Finnell

The Resource Foundation
Empowering Donors to Strengthen Communities

PROGRAMS

Affordable Housing

Every family deserves a dignified home. TRF's affiliates in five countries are helping families in need build simple, affordable, and dignified homes. Proven programs include prefabricated production of homes, sewage management, sidewalk construction, and tree planting, as well as many other services. For example, *SERVIVIENDA* in Colombia produces prefabricated model homes which are sturdy, attractive, easily transportable, and can be erected in four hours by the families that purchase them.

Capacity Building

Each year, The Resource Foundation organizes training seminars in the region to build the organizational capacity of its affiliates. In 2010, it sponsored a training seminar in Peru on how organizations can align human capital recruitment and retention strategies with their missions. The event featured experts from the World Bank, Enterprise Solutions to Poverty, and diverse NGOs. A total of 60 representatives of 40 organizations from Latin America and the Caribbean attended the seminar.

Cultural Programs

TRF helps to support an array of socially-relevant arts and cultural programs for disadvantaged children, youth and families. Supported projects include cultural centers, museums, and foundations that promote cultural preservation and provide access to art, science, and cultural works for all sectors of society. In Brazil, *CRIA* offers art and cultural activities such as theater, poetry, dance, and music to promote self-esteem, creativity, and social skills among at-risk youth.

Disaster Relief

In the aftermath of natural disasters, immediate responses and programs that address long-term needs are critical. TRF's affiliates have unparalleled expertise in meeting the pressing needs of affected children and families. By quickly assessing needs on the ground and providing immediate support, affiliates are able to help victims cope with the trauma, rebuild their homes, reestablish their businesses, and restore their livelihoods. For example, in response to the January 12th earthquake that devastated Haiti, TRF's affiliates provided food, shelter and clothing to survivors hours after the quake and have continued to provide counseling, training and support to facilitate their emotional, social and economic recovery.

*Learn more about
The Resource Foundation
Visit our website ...*

www.resourcefnd.org

176

The Resource Foundation
Empowering Donors to Strengthen Communities

PROGRAMS

Education and Job-Skills Training

To ensure that children and youth have access to superior educational programs and are equipped to successfully participate in the global economy, affiliates throughout the region are implementing a wide range of educational and job skills programs. *ORIGEN* in Chile and *FUNDAEC* in Colombia provide low-income and at-risk youth with an accredited high school degree. *UNETE* in Mexico provides training in computer skills for children enrolled in public schools, and *SUPERATEC* offers youths and adults in Venezuela the opportunity to acquire computer and personal development skills.

Environmental Concerns

TRF's affiliates combine environmental conservation with income-generating projects, such as plant and tree nurseries, sustainable fishing, and ecotourism. These innovative, cross-cutting initiatives prove that environmental protection and human progress are not mutually exclusive. For example, *FVSA* in Argentina and *SalvaNATURA* in El Salvador promote environmental conservation through education and ecological reserve management, while also promoting ecotourism projects to help community members generate increased income.

Health

In order to address today's complex health challenges, TRF's affiliates are implementing comprehensive health care and prevention programs. These include basic and preventive health care, reproductive and maternal and infant health, pediatric health care, HIV/AIDS prevention and care, cancer screenings, diabetes prevention, and others. For example, in Argentina, Fundación Huésped's provides direct services, training and education about HIV/AIDS and incorporates youth, adults and the elderly as multipliers, allowing them to share information with their peers so that they can be active in their health and well-being.

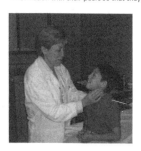

Learn more about
The Resource Foundation
Visit our website ...

www.resourcefnd.org

The Resource Foundation
Empowering Donors to Strengthen Communities

PROGRAMS

Microenterprise and Microfinance

Throughout Latin America and the Caribbean small family-owned businesses are important drivers of the economy as they offer jobs and generate incomes within communities. TRF's affiliates offer a range of microenterprise and financial training, technical assistance, and credit and sales services to improve microentrepreneurs' profits and ensure their long-term sustainability. In Peru, for example, *Grupo ACP* offers workshops and training sessions that enable micro and small business owners to apply modern business management techniques to commercial and financial activities. In El Salvador, *SalvaNATURA* provides environmental and entrepreneurial training to individuals living in border areas of a protected national park to make it possible for them to run successful eco-tourism businesses.

Potable Water and Sanitation

TRF's affiliates play an active role in addressing inadequate access to potable water and sanitation services for low-income, and especially rural communities. They install pipes, wells, and cost-effective water treatment plants, and provide training about water systems management. In addition, they offer training in health and hygiene to educate children and families about water-borne illness and sanitation measures. In Honduras, *Agua para Pueblo (APP)* works closely with community members to provide access to potable water and sanitation systems in order to improve health and living conditions.

Sustainable Agriculture

Small-scale farmers provide essential food supplies for the region's growing population, yet many farmers need training to improve their crop yields and generate a livelihood to support their families. TRF's affiliates manage sustainable agriculture programs that combine environmental education and protection with improved farming techniques. Programs teach water conservation and management, terrace farming, use of solar energy for greenhouses and homes, animal husbandry, and more. In Guatemala, *Fundación del Centavo* trains women in livestock and agricultural production to help them gain valuable Skills and increase their income.

Learn more about
The Resource Foundation
Visit our website ...
www.resourcefnd.org

178

Pilar and me.
And they said we would never last.

About the Author

Loren Finnell is the President, CEO and Founder of The Resource Foundation. He is a humanitarian, a pioneer, and a social entrepreneur with 47-years of experience working with nonprofit organizations (NGOs) worldwide. In 1987, he founded The Resource Foundation to leverage the resources and experience of donors worldwide, and NGOs in Latin America and the Caribbean to increase the self-reliance and living standards of the disadvantaged. He has been credited with "taking a leading role in making American development donors and practitioners focus on the needs of local NGOs," as well as "writing the book" on encouraging and helping individuals and corporations support the work of these agencies.

In honor of his life's work, The National Peace Corps Association selected Dr. Finnell to receive the 2006 Sargent Shriver Award for Distinguished Humanitarian Service at a ceremony in the Senate Caucus Room on Capitol Hill. He was designated to be a Skoll Foundation Fellow that same year. He has been honored three times by his alma mater, Manchester College, first for his philanthropic activity (1997), and followed by an Alumni Award (2002). He then received a Doctor of Humane Letters degree, honoris causa, and gave the commencement address at the May 2008 graduation exercises. In 2009, the Foreign Policy Association, the nation's oldest international affairs organization, invited him to become a Fellow. In 2011, he was invited to become a member of the Clinton Global Initiative.

Prior to establishing The Resource Foundation in 1987, Dr. Finnell headed his own consulting firm for eight years, supporting the programmatic and management needs of U.S., Canadian and developing world NGOs in Latin America, Africa and Asia, as well as fulfilling USAID contracts. From 1972 to 1979, Dr. Finnell helped found and develop Private Agencies Collaborating Together (PACT), a U.S.-based international consortium of NGOs, serving as its Deputy Executive Director and managing a Development Fund that made grants to development projects benefiting low-income individuals and families.

Dr. Finnell had two tenures with International Voluntary Services, as Program Director in Washington, DC (1971-72) and as Staff in Laos (1966-68) during the time of conflict. In the interim, he was Project Officer for the International Development Foundation, serving in Colombia and Ecuador. His international career began as a Peace Corps volunteer in Ecuador during 1964-66. Dr. Finnell has written numerous technical documents, reports and publications on management and programmatic issues facing NGOs worldwide. He has visited 44 countries in Latin America, Africa and Asia on multiple occasions, is fluent in Spanish and has a solid understanding of Portuguese.